EMBRACING AFFLICTIONS

EMBRACING AFFLICTIONS

Copyright © 2022 by Reverend Scott Eberle
ISBN: 9798819712016
All rights reserved.
First Printing, 2022, USA

This book or any portion thereof may not be reproduced or used in any manner whatsoever without the express written permission of the author, except for brief quotations in a book review. Unless otherwise specified, Scripture quotations are from The King James Version of the Bible, used under Fair Use. Scripture quotations marked NIV are from The Holy Bible, New International Version®, NIV® Copyright © 1973, 1978, 1984, 2011 by Biblica, Inc.™ Used by permission. All rights reserved worldwide.

TABLE OF CONTENTS

Foreword by Rev. Keith McKinnies — 4
Acknowledgements — 6
Preface — 8

My Conversion — 10

My Calling — 26

My Confusion — 35

My Comeback — 57

My Challenges — 85

My Calamity — 104

Embracing Afflictions — 122

FOREWORD

When I was asked to write this forward for my good friend, Scott Eberle, I was deeply honored. I've come to know him very well over the years, and find him to be a man of high morals, great integrity and honorable character. I've always said this many times about our friendship that God put us together. One notable attribute about him is that he is the same every day as he is in the pulpit. It's these type of men, in a world which is filled with such artificial life styles, that are needed to speak to us directly and honestly. We all truly need each other. I have watched Brother Eberle pastor his flock with gentleness and great understanding, treating everyone with respect.

When I started reading this book, I was not able to put it down. It starts with his conversion and how God found him. He knew nothing about the Apostolic doctrine, but his story shows you first-hand how God can take a person with a sincere heart and mold them into a great man of God. Along with his compassionate wife, Debbie, and his talented daughter Marissa, they have become great leaders in the Apostolic Church.

The book also talks of his struggles with health and life circumstances. We may not want to talk about our troubles, but we all have our personal giants that we need to face.

We find in the Word of God that Paul sought the Lord thrice to remove his infirmity, which He did not. He said, "Paul, My grace is sufficient." This shows you that all of us face difficult things, but that we should rely on God as Brother Eberle has done.

I hope you enjoy this book as you read of an incredible testimony of a life that was given to the Lord wholeheartedly, and that it would inspire you to share your own. For when it's all said and done, we all have a testimony to share.

Bishop Keith McKinnies

ACKNOWLEDGEMENTS

For well over 15 years, I've been saying that I should write a book. As I would write things in my journal over the years I actually imagined that one day it would be in a book form, but thinking about writing a book and actually doing it are two different things. I want to thank Anthony Miller for all of his expertise and encouragement in helping this book become a reality. I will never forget the day I was sharing my ideas with him and he responded with the simple words, "Let's do it". From that point on, he provided the confidence and the continued guidance that I needed, plus we shared plenty of laughs along the way. I also want to thank his wife Danielle for doing a second edit on the book and adding in some constructive criticism that made the book flow better. Anthony and Danielle together make a great team.

I want to thank Bishop Keith McKinnies for writing the forward to this book, but also for his undying encouragement over the years. As I state in the book, I look to him as my mentor, pastor, and one of my best friends, whom I love very much. I also want to give a special thanks to Sister Joyce McKinnies for providing me with the perfect title for this book.

To my precious daughter Marissa. Through all my struggles she always validates me living for God. When I stand back and listen to her speak, or sing, or play piano in church, it makes me so proud of the young lady that she has become. I can't wait to see all that God is going to do in her future. I love her with all of my heart.

Of course I can't go without acknowledging my precious wife Debbie. I cherish her friendship and what she means to me as a wife. As you read this book and listen to the story of my struggles don't forget, though at times unmentioned, she was always in the background as an encouragement. Sometimes she had words of wisdom. Other times she would pray with me. And other times she would just listen, but she was always there. I would not be the man I am today if it wasn't for her. Besides the Lord Jesus Christ, she is my greatest treasure in this whole world.

Most of all I want to thank the Lord Jesus Christ. In December of 1992, He pulled me out of the dark pit of sin and brought me into His marvelous light. He took a broken vessel and made me brand new. Without Him I might not be alive today, but through Him and because of Him I have a testimony. Without Him there would be no book to write. He is the author and the finisher of my faith. To Him I give all the glory!

Scott Eberle

PREFACE

Is any among you afflicted? The answer is an absolute yes! Today, ministers and laymen alike are suffering, and tragically many do so in silence. Sometimes we don't admit our struggles because we don't want to appear weak, or we simply don't think anyone will understand. Some of us have sought answers for the distresses of life only to be left with the same unanswered questions. Nevertheless, James felt an urging from the Holy Ghost to ask the question, "Is any one among you afflicted?" He then followed up with this word of encouragement:

> *"Let him pray."*
> James 5:13

This all sounds very simple: if you're afflicted - pray. Yet after being in the ministry for 27 years, I have learned that life's struggles are not always that easy. I wish they were, because it would be so wonderful to look into the eyes of an afflicted soul and tell them just to pray, and everything will be alright. I would love to think that a short season of prayer would fix all our problems. Don't misunderstand me: I am not discounting or diminishing the transforming power of prayer, but there are many factors to evaluate in the life of an afflicted soul. For instance, what is the root cause of the affliction? We can't blame everything on the devil, as sometimes we may be the cause of our own suffering. Maybe we need to change something in our life, or perhaps we need to learn how to live differently. Do we need to change our attitude, our perspective, our diet, our friends, or our approach to handling money?

I am writing to you from the perspective of a pastor who has suffered from his own mistakes as well as attacks of the enemy, but I've learned some incredible lessons along the way. This is the reason for writing: to discuss my suffering, my stress, and my struggles. Then, share with you how I have dealt with things the enemy would use to destroy me, and how God has made all things work together for my good. I pray that my story will help you.

* * * *

Are you afflicted?

CHAPTER ONE
MY CONVERSION

"And such were some of you: but ye are washed, but ye are sanctified, but ye are justified in the name of the Lord Jesus, and by the Spirit of our God."
1 Corinthians 6:11

I grew up in a normal, traditional American family; my parents both worked and I had a younger brother. Our parents took good care of us. We ate dinner together at the kitchen table every night; we went camping in the summer. My brother and I played sports. Everything was what you would call "good" or "normal", but we never went to church, and we didn't have a bible in the house, so I grew up without any knowledge of God or the need for salvation.

However, I can still remember my first prayer when I was around seven or eight years old. I knelt by my bedside one night and prayed, "God, if you're real, would you put a Mr. Potato Head under my bed while I sleep?" I got up off my knees and went to sleep. In the morning I eagerly jumped out of bed and looked under my bed... no Mr. Potato Head. Disappointed, I concluded at a young age that God must not be real, and I placed him in the same category as Bigfoot or the Lochness Monster. Case closed!

As a kid I loved football, and played through middle and high school. I dreamed of playing in college, and maybe even the NFL. What kid hasn't had those kinds of dreams? However, I found a new interest at the age of 16 - the electric guitar. Soon after I started playing guitar, my passion for football faded and a desire to be a guitarist consumed me. I took lessons for about a year, then began to teach myself. I advanced quickly and in about two years time I found myself teaching others to play at a local music store, where many of my students had been playing longer than me. I only taught at the music store for about a year, but during that time I decided that after graduating from high school I would devote my entire life to playing guitar. I left the music store for a part-time job at a grocery store, but my real passion and dream was to play professionally in a band. The path, for me, was the clearest it had ever been.

I was into hard rock and heavy metal. I would devote a minimum of three hours per day playing and practicing. When time permitted, I would spend up to eight hours mastering the craft. It was pretty insane when I think about it now, but this was my all-consuming dream. I played in several bands during the next few years, which exposed me to temptations everywhere. I actually began experimenting with drugs and alcohol in the 10th grade, due to peer pressure. I resisted at first, but eventually caved in. However, once I started playing in bands I was in the bars up to six nights per week, so my drug and alcohol use increased significantly. It was just so easy to do because it was so prevalent. I was 21 years old at this time.

When I was 25 years old I was playing in a bar when some musicians from another band came and approached me about trying out for their band, who played all original music. They were trying to replace their former guitarist who had moved to California to enroll in a guitar school. The band was searching for the best heavy metal guitarist in the state of Michigan, and they chose me. I don't know that I was the best but I was certainly flattered! I tried out for the spot and was immediately accepted in the band. During the next few months we played several shows, and somehow earned a recording contract. My dreams were starting to come true, I was excited, my hard work was paying off… but then came affliction.

I was with that band less than a year when I began to have trouble playing. When a guitarist plays too much he or she can feel some soreness or muscle fatigue in their forearms, just like with any type of exercise. With rest, this usually goes away. However, I noticed that the tendons in my left forearm were becoming very tight and resting was not helping. Playing was becoming increasingly difficult and painful. I connected with a surgeon who had studied at the Mayo Clinic, who performed surgery on my arm. He cut open the tendon sheath, which encases the tendons, in hopes of releasing tension. A few weeks later I went back to playing and it seemed to have worked, but then the tendonitis came back worse than before. To complicate matters, I started having trouble with my right arm also. Things got so bad I was forced to lay down the guitar permanently.

This couldn't be happening, could it? My dreams were crumbling before my very eyes. Everyday I would wake up to what seemed like a bad dream. My guitar would just sit there in the corner as if it was mocking me. I ended up giving my guitar away to a friend of mine because I couldn't stand to look at it any longer.

Even though I had stopped playing guitar, the tendonitis in both arms continued to worsen and became chronic to the point of being placed on workers' compensation. It was a daily chore to shave and comb my hair, let alone drive or work a job. I wore wrist braces constantly to help alleviate the discomfort, but nothing really worked. I was miserable. I sought out help from every place I could think of. I went to the University of Michigan Comprehensive Hand Center, and met the chief surgeon. He told me he was not a magician and that I would have to learn to live with the pain. Unhappy with that answer, my mother and I took a train to the Mayo Clinic in Minnesota, where we spent a few days. I endured much testing only for them to send me home with no answers. I felt hopeless, because Mayo Clinic is supposed to have some of the best doctors in the world, yet, they could not help me.

I recall writing in my journal, "Dreams are like promises, they are not meant to be broken... but often they are." Everywhere you look in life you'll find people with broken dreams. You may be reading this and be suffering with your own broken dreams. What do you do when life does not turn out as you expected? How do you go on? In my case, I now realize I was depressed and grieving what I had lost. Grieving may sound like a strong word but believe me its not. Something in me had died and I felt like life was over. Little did I know that my life was just starting to take shape. God had a plan for my life, and all of this affliction was the tool He was using to redirect my steps. Ps 119:67 says, *"Before I was afflicted I went astray: but now have I kept thy word."* I did not know I was straying from God. How could I? I didn't even know that God existed, but He knew me. God was about to change me in a drastic way, setting me up for a life-changing experience and revelation that would forever transform me.

When people are in pain, they more easily sense a void in their lives. Unfortunately, they usually don't know what is causing it or how to satisfy it. This is why so many turn to drugs, alcohol, or pornography as a coping mechanism. Some choose other pursuits, like being workaholics or simply immersing everything they have into their career. The enemy of our souls wants to blind, bind, and take the life out of us. Satan is a cruel and evil taskmaster and a master of deception. It may look good outwardly, but the gnawing pain and void of a life without God persists. Many have become adept at hiding behind facades of success and phony smiles, but they are inwardly craving what only God can supply. When Jesus met the woman at the well she had been married and divorced five times, and was with a sixth man. She came to the well to get water for her physical thirst, but Jesus knew that what she really needed was a well on the inside. She was a broken soul that had too often encountered the unfairness of life, which had left her depleted and defeated. Jesus offered her living water: He said that it would be like a well of water on the inside that would spring up into everlasting life. Today, we call this well the Holy Ghost. When she heard his message she dropped her water-pot and ran to tell people about Jesus. He was the seventh man in her life, and He quenched the relentless thirst of her soul, making her truly complete for the first time in her life. What we all need is not drugs, alcohol, pornography, another relationship, more money, more success, or even another church service. Only Jesus can satisfy the soul!

Now there I was in my late-twenties, plagued with tendonitis, haunted by shattered dreams, and wallowing in loneliness. I was in the pit of affliction. One day my parents attended a business meeting at a home of nearby friends. When they returned they excitedly announced that they had become Amway distributors and that it was a great way to make extra money. Becoming an Amway distributor involves buying your products through the Amway corporation instead of going to a local store. You then recruit others to do likewise. It's called multi-level marketing. Amway pays you based on how much product is sold through you, and some have become quite wealthy doing so. They encouraged me to attend the next meeting. I had nothing to lose so I thought, "Why not?" The next thing I knew I had become an Amway distributor. I never made enough money to quit my grocery store job, but it was a way to supplement my income. I found out that several of the people associated with this group were part of a family of Baptists, and I silently told myself that if they ever invited me to church or talked about Jesus I would quit the business. I wanted nothing to do with anything or anyone religious.

To my amazement they never brought up church or Jesus. Instead, they did something that deeply affected me: they loved and accepted me for who I was. I was described as nice, but was very rough around the edges. I had long hair hanging halfway down my back and my manners were never the greatest. I avoided using profanity around them, but I'm sure they knew that wasn't the real me. Oliver Goldsmith once said, "You can preach a better sermon with your life than with your lips," and that's exactly what they did. Jesus said we are to be as light and salt in our world. Light illuminates and salt preserves, but neither can speak. This was their approach, and it worked. Without saying a word, I could feel the love of God through them. It was breaking down my defenses and I felt truly safe around them. This is because God's love never condemns others. I can imagine that the woman caught in adultery felt both safe *and* guilty in the presence of Jesus at the same time. This atmosphere is where true repentance can take root.

The Amway business held out of state functions a few times each year. They were scheduled on the weekend, and usually took place in large auditoriums where we heard famous motivational speakers who were hired to inspire us. On Sunday mornings there were optional non-denominational church services. I loved the functions, but avoided those church services like the plague. One particular weekend, however, the people that I was riding with decided to stay for the service and I had no way to avoid attending. I remember entering a 10,000 seat auditorium where I sat way back on the balcony. When the worship started I saw people standing and lifting their hands to God and giving Him praise. I had never seen anything like that, but it felt so beautiful. The preacher soon came to the pulpit, but he was so distant that I couldn't even make out his features. I can't tell you who he was, but as he preached I was simply captivated. I felt like he was preaching directly to me! I thought to myself, "How does he know my inner secrets? Has he hired a private investigator to follow me around?" That day, the seed of God's word was planted in my heart. When I walked out of that service I instinctively knew that one day I would be a Christian, but had no idea how that would happen.

> *"Being born again, not of corruptible seed,*
> *but of incorruptible, by the word of God,*
> *which liveth and abideth forever."*
> 1 Peter 1:23

Despite not growing up in church I was not completely ignorant of Jesus. From kids at school or religious programs on television, I had heard the stories about His birth, the cross, and the resurrection. I just had no clue why He was relevant. I'd had people tell me that I needed to be saved. My question was always saved from what? From my view I was alright. Why would I want to be a church person? They all seemed so starchy, so formal. They had so many things that they couldn't do, while I was free to do as I pleased. Now, however, I was becoming attracted to the kinds of people I had always avoided, and started avoiding the people I had always hung out with. The Lord was changing my appetite for life from the carnal to the spiritual.

Once I got back home from the Amway conference, I started a new ritual of Bible reading. Every evening I would walk down to the corner party store and buy a quart of beer and go home and read my bible. That's right, a beer in one hand, a bible in the other! One night I felt a little guilty about the beer so I searched in the bible's concordance. I couldn't find beer mentioned in the bible, only Beersheba. Then I found scriptures that said that wine is a mocker, and not to be drunk with wine. So I came to a feeble conclusion that wine was to be avoided, but beer was okay. Isn't it funny how we can justify things we don't want to give up? Don't worry. God eventually took care of the beer drinking.

Jesus said that when the Holy Ghost came He would convict the world of sin. Conviction is God's loving way of helping us to repent of our sins, and never go back. Because of this I eventually laid down the beer for good. This is why Paul said that "by grace are you saved through faith; and not of yourselves: it is the gift of God. Not of works, lest any man should boast". Grace, according to Strong's Concordance, means "the divine influence upon the heart". In other words, God graciously influences people to repent, but people have to respond to that grace, and not resist. The grace of God told Noah to build an ark to save his house. Had Noah disobeyed, he and his family would have perished, but that would have been on Noah, not God. The Lord is not willing that any should perish, but that all should come to repentance. It's amazing that so many people resist this loving God that is trying to save them from hell.

Jesus is a liberator who sets sinners free from the guilt, shame and the condemnation of sin. He's our strength when we are weak, our joy in sorrow, our peace in the storm, and our light in the darkness. When the prophet Moses asked

God for His name He said, "I Am That I Am". In other words, I am whatever you need me to be. Like Andre Crouch sang many years ago, "Jesus is the answer for the world today. Above Him there's no other, Jesus is the way."

Nine months after I began reading the Bible came the month of December, 1992, which will forever be etched in my memory. At 28 years old, tendonitis was still a problem for me. My workers' compensation benefits at the grocery store had run out, so I was forced to go back to work with restrictions. I worked there with a lady named Sharon who also held a job at a daycare, where Debbie was employed. One day while I was working Debbie came into the grocery store and Sharon said to her, "What are you doing here, Debbie? Are you looking for a husband? Stay right there, I've got just the guy for you." Sharon quickly came and got me and said, "Scott, I have someone I want you to meet." Sharon introduced us and the rest is history. We only spoke a few words to each other as we were both a little shy, but there was an instant chemistry. Debbie later told me that she went home and actually wrote a letter to one of her friends and said, "I just met my husband today." Right away we started dating, and two months later, on Valentine's Day, we were engaged to be married. Six months later, we were married!

Debbie was raised in church, but I was not. Before I met Debbie I was reading a little booklet on prayer, that explained how to pray and have your prayers answered. It said to ask the Father in Jesus' name for whatever you needed, and then to thank Him as if it was already done. So, every day on my way to work I would pray a little prayer that went like this: "Father I ask you in the name of Jesus that you would give me a wife, and I thank You for giving me a wife in Jesus' name." Two weeks after I started that prayer, I met Debbie. This is why I always tell people that yes, she is an answer to my prayers.

The same month that I met Debbie, after coming home from doing an Amway presentation, I gave my life to Christ. Lyle, a business associate of mine, was with me. He was 30 years older than me, had a genuine love for people, a witty sense of humor, and an infectious laugh. When he entered a room he made people feel better. He was also very strong in his faith, and belonged to a Baptist church. That particular day he was driving me home and I blurted out, "Lyle, I need some religion in my life". He asked if I had a Bible in the house. I said I did, and he came in and began teaching me some scriptures. I stopped him and asked, "What do I need to do to be saved?" He told me that I needed to believe that Jesus died for my sins and was raised from the dead three days later, and that I needed to repent and ask Jesus to forgive me of my sins and to save my soul. Sitting at a kitchen table he helped me to pray, and I felt the beautiful presence of the Holy Ghost come all over me. Miraculously, it felt like a thousand pounds had been lifted off of my mind, and I felt the peace of God that surpasses all understanding consume me. What a wonderful day that was! God was just starting to bless me.

Soon after my conversion I woke up with sciatic nerve pain in my hip. I told my dad about it and he suggested that I see his chiropractor. During my visit to the chiropractor, he asked me why I was wearing braces on both of my wrists. I told him about my three-year battle with tendonitis and how I had failed to find any relief. After a short examination, he discovered that the vertebrae in my neck were out of alignment and pinching on the nerves, which caused the pain and the tightness in my tendons. He adjusted my neck and I felt immediate relief. It was so amazing, and I continued to get adjustments three times a week for the next few months. Gradually the vertebrae in my neck begin to stay in place, and the achiness, pain, and tightness in my tendons subsided. I was able to throw away the wrist braces. I don't think it's a coincidence that my healing came *after* I had repented.

According to His wisdom, God can and will use affliction to get our attention and cause us to pray and seek His face. Once affliction has accomplished its purpose, it goes away.

Consider the following scriptures:

*"I will go and return to my place,
till they acknowledge their offense, and seek my face:
in their affliction they will seek me early."*
Hosea 5:15.

"Then Jonah prayed unto the Lord his God out of the fish's belly, and said, I cried by reason of mine affliction unto the Lord, and he heard me; out of the belly of Hell cried I, and thou heardest my voice."
Jonah 2:1-2

"And she was in bitterness of soul, and prayed unto the Lord, and wept sore. And she vowed a vow, and said, oh lord of hosts, if thou wilt indeed look on the affliction of thine handmaid and remember me…"
1 Samuel 1:10-11

In my case, I believe God allowed the affliction of tendonitis to get a hold of my heart. Affliction took the guitar out of my hands, and got me in God's hands. Please don't misunderstand me: God in no way is against guitar playing, but my guitar playing was so entangled with a life of sin that it had to go. Without God's intervention, there was no way I would ever part with my guitar. It was a part of me and laying it down was like suffering an amputation, but that temporary affliction saved me from eternal torment.

You may wonder if I ever picked up the guitar again. A few years ago, I did purchase a guitar and I do play a little, but not like I used to. Instead, I now play just for my own enjoyment. If I play too much, the tendonitis wants to creep back. This reminds me of when God took Jacob's hip out of joint and he limped for the rest of his life. Pain was actually God's way of blessing Jacob. One preacher described it as, "the limp that won't leave." Hebrews 11:21 says, "*By faith Jacob, when he was dying... worshipped, leaning upon the top of his staff.*" The limp and the worship went together. Our "limp" is what makes us need God. Every worshiper has a limp that won't leave, but neither will the presence of God. What's your limp? A limp causes us to walk with difficulty. You may ask why is your walk with God so difficult, and it may seem like no one else struggles like you. Believe me, every Christian has their struggles, and the problem is that we just don't openly discuss them. 1 Peter 5:9 mentions, "*The same afflictions are accomplished in your brethren that are in the world.*" The NIV Bible states it this way: "*You know that the family of believers throughout the world is undergoing the same kind of sufferings.*"

Acts 7:9-10 says, "*And the Patriarchs, moved with Envy, sold Joseph into Egypt: but God was with him, and delivered him out of all **his afflictions**, and gave him a favor and wisdom and the sight of pharaoh king of Egypt; and he **made him** Governor over Egypt and all his house.*"

Notice the words that I put in bold letters: **"his afflictions...made him."** I'm convinced that it was not Joseph's dreams that made him a great leader, it was his afflictions: the pit, his brothers' hatred, Potiphar's wife and her false accusations, slavery, and spending time in the prison. These experiences shaped his character, which in turn, prepared him to step into the reality of his dreams.

In my life I can clearly see that God allowed affliction to bring me to where I am today, and I can wholeheartedly echo the words of the psalmist David:

> *"It is good for me that I have been afflicted;*
> *that I might learn thy statutes."*
> Psalm 119:71

CHAPTER TWO
MY CALLING

*"Now therefore go, and I will be with thy mouth,
and teach thee what thou shalt say."*
Exodus 4:12

Reverend E.B. Andrews pastored the Apostolic Lighthouse in Vandercook Lake, Michigan, from 1982 until he passed away in 2013. If anyone ever loved Jesus with all of their heart, soul, mind, and strength it was him. Pastor Andrews worked as an Archway Cookie delivery man, and his route would always take much longer than expected because he would stop and tell anyone that would listen about Jesus and the Plan of Salvation. At the height of his ministry the gifts of healing flowed freely in his life, and many people were healed instantly when he laid hands on them in the name of Jesus Christ. If you met him in public and requested prayer, he would stop what he was doing and pray for you right there, on-the-spot. He loved his God and was not ashamed of his faith. He was also Debbie's grandfather, and after we started dating, she invited me to his church where I began to experience the power of the Holy Ghost.

I remember one service in particular where Pastor Andrews had called somebody to the front for prayer, and as he laid his hands on them, the glory of God filled that little church. There was a cross on the back wall of the platform that literally began to glow, but to my knowledge, no one else saw it but me. It reminds me of Daniel 10:8 which says, *"And I Daniel alone saw the vision: For the men that were with me saw not the vision."* God can reveal something to one person that another person may not see, and I firmly believe that he was revealing his glory to me at that moment. At one point I felt like my body was being lifted up off the ground, so I looked down to see if my feet were still on the ground and I was thankful that they were! In that church I found out just how real the presence of God is for myself, and I am so grateful for those experiences! I learned that Jesus is not just a Bible character, or a great teacher who lived two thousand years ago. Jesus is very much alive today and manifests himself to people through the power of the Holy Ghost. He is the same yesterday, today, and forever!

When I met Pastor Andrews, he was already in his mid-70s, had suffered a stroke, and had been praying for a ministry partner in the church. Little did I know that I was soon to be that partner. In my mind, I was only there to attend church and grow as a Christian… of course it didn't hurt that I was falling in love with his granddaughter, which was always a motivation to attend church. Pastor Andrews would preach Acts 2:38 and the need to be baptized in Jesus' name for the remission of sins, and then the need for receiving the gift of the Holy Ghost. It was only a few short weeks later that I was baptized, fully immersed in water, in the precious name of our Lord and savior Jesus Christ.

During that time, members of the church kept talking to me about the experience and necessity of being filled with the Holy Ghost. They taught me that when a person is filled with the Holy Ghost, it will be accompanied with the sign of tongue-speaking. This can be plainly seen throughout the scriptures; for your reference: *Acts 2:1-4, Acts 10:44-48, and Acts 19:1-7.* Tongue-speaking is God's idea, not man's, and it still belongs in the church today! I began seeking earnestly to be filled with the gift of the Holy Ghost and it happened in the month of May, 1993. I remember it vividly: I was at home, kneeling by my bedside, praying. As I was about to say something in English, suddenly the Lord took my tongue and I found myself speaking in another language. I excitedly got up off my knees and I remember doing a little dance right there in the bedroom. As I continued to praise the Lord, I spoke in tongues again, in a second language distinctly different from the first. I was 29 years old, and overjoyed with my full salvation experience! A few short months later, Debbie and I were married.

After receiving the Holy Ghost, some people may have a season or trial when they doubt. We may wonder if it is really God that spoke through us, or if we just had some strange experience that we conjured up through the power of imagination. That question was soon put to rest for me, when Debbie and I, as newlyweds, were invited to a home prayer meeting. We arrived a few minutes late and walked into a living room where the prayer meeting was in full swing. I remember speaking in tongues during that prayer meeting and afterward, my mother-in-law who was bilingual, said that I was praying in perfect Spanish over my father, mother, and brother... and I didn't know any Spanish. There is no way possible that a person could speak in gibberish and just happen to pick the right words from a foreign language they'd never been taught. This lets you know that the Holy Ghost is the intelligence of God. Isaiah 40:13 says, *"Who hath directed the spirit of the Lord, or being his counselor hath taught him?"* If a person wants to learn how to speak a foreign language they have to go to school and spend at least a semester in study. Yet God can teach somebody to speak another language in a split second! We should never mock or make fun of the power of the Holy Ghost.

Pastor Andrews would occasionally ask me to lead the song service on Sunday evenings, which involved standing behind the pulpit and announcing page numbers from the hymnal. I was nervous, yet honored. I was growing spiritually by leaps and bounds and about one year after receiving the Holy Ghost, I felt the call of God into the ministry. I was walking through my in-laws living room when the Lord suddenly dropped a word in my spirit. I quickly grabbed my Bible, a pen and paper, and began to write down the thoughts that the Lord had impressed upon my heart. I went to church that next Sunday evening and told Pastor Andrews that I felt that the Lord had given me a message. He kindly allowed me to preach it to the congregation. It only lasted about fifteen minutes, but there was a flow to it and it made sense.

I never in my wildest dreams wanted to be a preacher. In the seventh grade I had actually skipped speech class. On the day I was scheduled to speak, I was so terrified that I decided that it would be better to take a failing grade than to have to stand before my peers to speak. I think God must have a sense of humor when He chooses people to serve him. In the scriptures, Moses and Jeremiah were both reluctant to speak for God, but God enabled them in spite of their excuses. In 2nd Corinthians 3:5-6 the Apostle Paul said, "*Our sufficiency is of God. Who also hath made us able ministers of the New Testament.*" It's been said that public speaking is one of the greatest fears of man. It is interesting to me that when God gave me that first message, I was so moved by the anointing that I forgot about all of the fears I once had.

Immediately after preaching my first message, Pastor Andrews allowed me to preach every Sunday evening, meanwhile he continued teaching Sunday School. Those poor people were so patient with me in my early days. I had the anointing, but I was far from wise. I was just a young guy full of fire and ready to give it everything I had. One neighboring pastor said facetiously, "If we could just get Brother Eberle excited..."

Preaching the Word of God is vastly different than playing a musical instrument, but it requires the same level of devotion if you are going to succeed, which I suppose is true in any vocation or calling. I didn't want to be just an average preacher, or even a good preacher... I wanted to be a great preacher. I hope that doesn't sound arrogant; I believe that we can be zealous and humble at the same time. On the cross Jesus gave his best for us, and I believe that we in turn should give our best for him. Romans 12:1 says, *"Present your bodies a living sacrifice, holy, acceptable unto God, which is your reasonable service."*

With that being said, I realize that all preachers have their own unique giftings, and some will have a greater impact than others. In the parable of the talents, Jesus spoke of men being given one, two, and five talents respectively. Not every preacher will become another Jeff Arnold, Lee Stoneking, or an Anthony Mangun. Likewise, not every pastor is called to pastor a large church. Regardless of status, visibility, or average church attendance, none of us are insignificant. Any work for God is great, and some of the greatest men you will ever meet pastor some of the smallest churches. When we answer God's call and develop whatever giftings He has deposited in us, it is pleasing to Him.

My newfound passion and excitement that I now had for the ministry reminded me of how I had once felt about guitar playing. I remember thinking to myself that in order to be a great guitar player, I had to devote hours each day practicing my technique and learning everything I could. So, I decided to do likewise with the ministry. Every day I would spend hours locked in a room praying, studying, and worshiping God. I was utterly consumed. This was in 1994, and I was just 30 years old.

I was on my way: anointed, prayerful, zealous, committed, disciplined, and sincerely in love with God. My motives were pure; I wasn't in it for money or fame; I was open to correction, but there was a problem that would eventually catch up with me... I was out of balance. A person without balance is heading for a fall, and I was missing one essential ingredient that is vital in the life of every Christian, especially those in ministry. That ingredient was and still is rest.

Many in Christendom view rest as slothfulness. I heard a story of a young man in Bible college who told his professor that when he became a pastor he would never take a day off because the devil doesn't take time off. The professor wisely responded, "Whose example are you going to follow, the devil's, or God's?"

In our movement, we teach that the Sabbath of the Old Testament is only a shadow of what is offered to us in the

New Testament. For Israel, it was only a physical and temporal rest, but for us it is a spiritual and eternal rest. We teach that the rest comes through the baptism of the Holy Ghost. I agree with that theology, but it does not mean that a saved person no longer needs physical rest. An automobile today can be driven well over 200,000 miles, but not all at once. I believe the only reason that the Prophet Elijah ran from Jezebel is because he was tired. After doing all those exploits: confronting false prophets, praying down fire from heaven, and praying a rainstorm into existence, he was out of balance. When he requested that God would take his life, God didn't rebuke him, but rather sent an angel with food and drink and let him sleep. You and I can fast 40 days and pray until our tongue polishes our shoes, but we still need to sleep and rest. The promise of a glorified body is for the next dispensation, not now.

I am writing from a pastor's perspective, but this can apply to all believers. When our life is out of balance it not only can affect our health, but our relationships as well. I will never forget when my daughter's school held its fifth grade graduation ceremony. In a large auditorium they dimmed the lights, and played a slideshow with music. I watched as they showed pictures that extended from kindergarten through the fifth grade, and within fifteen minutes, my little girl's life flashed before my eyes. Don't misread what I'm about to say. I have a wonderful relationship with my daughter, Marissa; but when that fifth grade graduation was over I went home and sobbed over missed memories and opportunities. I wonder how many things I missed in her life because I was too busy trying to be a pastor. I made a promise to myself that when she graduated from high school I would not have the same regrets. I'm happy to say that I kept that promise to myself and to her. I've since learned that love is spelled t-i-m-e.

If we as pastors and ministers are not careful, we can gain a ministry but lose our family. This is not God's will, and we must be diligent in being well-rounded. If you are in ministry, God wants you to enjoy your spouse and your children. They are your first calling; the most important part of your ministry.

I didn't know it at the time, but I was heading for a fall.

CHAPTER THREE
MY CONFUSION

*"For God is not the author of confusion,
but of peace, as in all churches of the saints."*
1 Corinthians 14:33

1999 was a year of blessings for myself and our church. I received my ordination license from the Assemblies of Our Lord Jesus Christ, Michigan District, and our church attendance doubled in the span of just a few months. Our little church building in Vandercook Lake, Michigan was packed out every Sunday night. There was much talk among church members about the need for a larger building, and that was an extremely exciting time for all of us.

Over the next three years, things went smoothly, but I was still pushing myself too hard and not resting. I can remember a few times feeling tired and just attributed it to the fact that I was getting older. For the most part, I felt strong physically, mentally, emotionally and spiritually. Preaching and praying was very easy for me - I felt invincible and unstoppable. I thought, "What could possibly hinder me?"

To supplement my income I started working a part-time job at a mall doing customer service, which was basically a security position. Around this same time, Pastor Andrews had allowed me to take over all of the preaching duties. Preaching three services per week, coupled with a part-time job, was a heavy load to carry, but I tried to do it the best I could. During the week, I devoted every spare moment I had to prayer and study. On Sundays I would always push myself to spend at least three hours in prayer between the morning and the evening service. I preached hard in those days, and always worked the altar. It was normal for me to pray for everybody in the church that I could get my hands on. This was my Sunday routine for years. I was still young and energy didn't seem to be a problem. Not yet.

In the Fall of 2001, I was invited to be one of the speakers at our ALJC District Conference. I preached a message entitled, "Is Any Among You Afflicted?", based on James 5:13. The word afflicted in Greek means, "*to undergo hardship or suffer trouble.*" This poses the question, is any among you undergoing hardship? Are any among you suffering trouble? If so, James said, "Let him pray". I spent a great deal of time in that message preaching about the power and the need to pray through our afflictions. I then brought up the question regarding people that have prayed for weeks, months, and possibly years... and yet the affliction persists. What then?

James 5:11 says, "Ye have heard of the patience of Job." Job suffered the type of affliction that makes most of us shudder. Can you imagine being completely destroyed financially, plus losing all of your children in the course of one day? Then a short time later suffering a sickness that leaves you with boils that cover your entire body? In addition, your spouse tells you to curse God and die, and your so-called friends turn against you and accuse you of being a hypocrite who has committed some secret sin.

Keep in mind that Job was not aware of the conversation that had ensued between God and Satan. He did not know anything about God in his sovereignty allowing Satan to attack him, nor did he know of the restrictions that God had placed on Satan. I wonder if he was anxious about when and where the next attack would take place?

In Job chapter 23, he began to pray and seek God for answers, but he failed to even find the presence of God. How discouraging! What do you do when prayer doesn't seem to work? In Job 23:10 he concluded, "*But he knows the way that I take, and when he has tried me, I shall come forth as gold.*" The word patience in the Greek language means, "*cheerful (or hopeful) endurance.*" I don't know how cheerful Job could have possibly been, but he was certainly hopeful and endured. The man must have had perseverance in his DNA. He never suffered from the dreaded disease called give-up-itis. Too many people give up because they think God has written the last chapter of their story and there is nowhere else to go. That's a lie from the pits of hell.

Satan is not the author and finisher of our faith. We need to keep getting up and continue living for God until He writes our next chapter.

I closed my message by suggesting that Jesus was perhaps the greatest example we have on how to endure affliction. He went with his disciples into a place called Gethsemane to pray prior to his crucifixion. I'm convinced that Jesus felt the weight of His cross mentally and emotionally long before He ever carried the cross physically. Peter, James, and John witnessed Him becoming sorrowful and very heavy. He was suffering before the nails were ever driven into His hands and feet, before the crown of thorns pierced His skull, before He ever suffered thirst, before He was ever whipped and beaten, spit upon, mocked, or ridiculed. In Matthew 26:39, we read, *"and he went a little further, and fell on his face, and prayed."* Eventually, an angel appeared from heaven and strengthened Him.

Most of the people in that service were ministers and their wives. When I gave the altar call I encouraged them to go a little further and fall on their face and pray, believing that they would receive strength from Heaven, whether by an angel or from the hand of God himself. I was amazed as the pews emptied and almost every minister came forward and fell down on their face at the altar. I didn't expect that and to be honest it shocked me as a real-life demonstration of just how much suffering goes unacknowledged in the church. Many pastors and their wives were bleeding while they were feeding. This was a powerful and moving experience.

After the service I was approached by our District Superintendent, Pastor Richard Curton. He said, "*Brother Eberle, God's got His hand on you and the devil knows it.*" That encouraged me as a young preacher, but I also took his words as an admonition to be watchful of the enemy. His words still ring in my ears today. In retrospect, they were strangely prophetic.

In 2002 I entered a season of afflictions with health battles that would continue for many years to come. In fact, I still have health challenges as I'm writing this book some 20 years later. It's amazing to me that I've been able to keep going. I've had numerous days of frustration, struggle, discouragement, stress, and I've felt just completely worn out. I still have a lot of questions that have been left unanswered by the medical community, and God himself. Yet I keep going because I know beyond a shadow of a doubt that God is with me, giving me strength when I need it most. I'm writing this book to let you know that no matter what you're going through, God can get you through it. I can't complain, instead I give God all the glory and the praise. It's His faithfulness that has brought me this far.

I kept a journal throughout most of my health battles. I'm going to share with you something I wrote in 2008, that reflects back on what started in 2002. I have not edited it except for some brief punctuation and a few additional words to make it more readable.

Journal Entry 11/8/2008:
"June 7 - 9, 2002, I preached three days of Revival services for brother Stephen Trachsel. It was then that I began a long and wearisome journey of stress, anxiety, depression and fatigue. I was dizzy that weekend and tense. Little did I know I would battle the physical and emotional symptoms of stress for years to come. At times I thought I was fighting demons, but in truth it was just my mind and body reacting to the stress of life.

July 6, 2002, the Lord spoke to me. It was a Saturday afternoon in a hotel in Taylor, Michigan. I was scheduled to preach for brother Mark Dunlap in the morning, and I was so depleted that I didn't have the strength to pray. When I did pray my body felt so tense, and my emotions were so edgy. This was perplexing to me because I had always been able to find a fresh anointing in prayer. I had learned that if I was anxious or afraid I could simply pray and get in the spirit, and the Lord would give me a boldness. But now, prayer seems stressful. I have since learned that sometimes when we find ourselves weary from the journey, God wants us to rest in him and wait patiently.

So I laid on the hotel bed that day and held the Bible to my heart. I prayed, Lord, I don't understand what's going on with me. Please speak to me. Then I opened the Bible and said, in Jesus' name. My eyes fell upon Jeremiah 30:17, which declares, "for I will restore Health unto thee." Overjoyed, I thanked Jesus and began expecting my healing.

After I had finished preaching the following morning I had some brothers from the church lay hands on me, and I expected to receive my healing. But it was not yet to be. God had some things He needed to teach me. I had no idea that I would suffer the horrible symptoms of anxiety, depression and fatigue for over six years.

A few times I have thought of the suffering of King Nebuchadnezzar. God Afflicted him for seven years so He could humble him. I wonder - will I have to endure seven years?

I must admit that my suffering has humbled me. I used to be filled with such pride. When I listen back to messages I preached six years ago I have to turn them off. What's strange is how blind I was to my condition back then. I've learned that I must decrease and He must increase. He alone is my sufficiency."

On July 24th, 2002, I visited the William R. Starr Camp and Conference Center, where the Michigan District UPCI was holding services. I cannot tell you who the speaker was that night, I just remember that I was a wreck. My soul felt as dry as a corn cob. The message that night was about David during his season of backsliding. The text came from Psalm 51, which is David's prayer of repentance. The message was entitled, "The Unforgettable Anointing". It spoke of how David, because of his sin, had lost his anointing and was praying that God would restore it back to him with joy. That message hit me like a ton of bricks because I felt that I had lost my anointing. I began to wonder - was I backslidden? Had I unknowingly sinned against God? Whatever it was, I was miserable.

On Wednesday, August 14th, 2002, I was scheduled to be the morning speaker at the ALJC camp meeting. I was already nervous and felt like I had lost my anointing, then my daughter and I got sick. I must have consumed half a bottle of Pepto-Bismol that week. It was terrible. The morning I was scheduled to preach I had two messages in mind, but had not felt strong enough to pray, and really didn't know which one to preach. It wasn't until I stepped to the pulpit that I felt the Holy Ghost give me direction. I preached a message entitled, "The Kingdom is Worth Dying For". In spite of feeling so terrible and not feeling prepared, I preached like I had been praying and fasting. I was strong and my anointing returned. After the service, my symptoms of sickness completely vanished for the rest of the week. I think the enemy was trying to mess with me, but God always comes through on time. God was trying to teach me that if I would rely more on Him, and not push myself so much, He would show up in my ministry.

2003 proved to be no better for me than 2002. My symptoms of stress continued. My mind was frazzled and my nerves were on edge. I had always enjoyed studying the word and preparing sermons, but now there were days it became a chore. I found a scripture in Ecclesiastes 12:12, which says, "*much study is a weariness of the flesh*". The word "weariness" in the Hebrew language means fatigue. The New Living Translation says, "*Much study wears you out.*" I mentioned that scripture to a pastor in our city and he chuckled, but I was dead serious. Of course, he had no idea what I was struggling with. Nevertheless, I kept pushing myself. I was seriously out of balance.

We can be struggling inwardly and yet look good outwardly. People can't see the battles that rage in our mind, emotions, and nervous systems, but God knows.

At an ALJC District Conference I was voted to serve on the District Board as a sectional presbyter. It was an honor, but I did not feel ready. Later I remember conducting a meeting with the ministers in our section and thinking - how can I lead a group of men when I can't seem to even organize and rule my own mind and emotions? I was the one that needed leadership. It was a confusing time for me.

By the end of 2003 our church had found a new building to relocate in. It would give us more than enough room, but would require about ten months of renovation, which we mostly did ourselves. It was exciting, but I didn't need more responsibility and pressure.

If we continue to push ourselves, our adrenal glands release stress hormones, such as adrenaline and cortisol. These hormones increase our heart rate, elevate our blood pressure and boost energy supplies. Living off the stress response can be addicting, like a drug, and that's why it can be so hard to slow down and unwind. It takes time, and the stressed-out person doesn't feel like they have time.

"When the body and mind are consistently overworked, it results in something that Dr. Richard Swenson calls "torque". Compare it to a tire swing on a tree, spun until the rope is tight. Add the weight of stress to it, and the rope likely will break. *'Healthy rest comes when we allow our high degree of torque to completely unwind,'* Swenson says. *'But when torque is at too high a level, it requires an extended period to come down to a restful baseline. Torque isn't easily switched off like a light switch. It only backs off slowly. Many people are wound so tightly they can take months or even years to unwind.'"* (Graves, 2001)[1].

---

1) Excerpt from *The Hard Work of Rest*, by Steven R. Graves

On Sunday, January 11th, 2004 came my breaking point. It happened in the late afternoon as I was preparing to preach the evening service.

I always preach my messages to the Lord before I preach them to the congregation. I like to feel after the spirit and see if God approves of the message. If I feel His anointing, then I know I have the right message. I was feeling good that day, but as I was preaching my message to the Lord I suddenly felt a sharp pain rip across the left side of my chest muscle. I became winded and a little disoriented. I sat down and felt very weak. I thought for sure I was having a heart attack. I was in the basement and I was worried about getting up the steps to tell my wife what had happened. After sitting there awhile I found the strength to get up and go upstairs. I would later realize that I had suffered a panic attack.

It was all very strange to me because I wasn't panicked or afraid about anything. I was simply pushing myself too hard and something in my body gave out. When I got to the church that evening I stood and told the congregation I did not have the strength to preach, so I simply spoke my message. I felt exhausted afterward.

Two days later, I was still experiencing some slight discomfort in my chest. It felt like the muscle had been bruised. I went to our new church building that we were renovating and tried to work, barely making it an hour before going back home. My heart rate was elevated; I was feeling weak and light headed.

The next day I went to see my doctor, and he prescribed Xanax for stressful times. He said he was 99% sure I had no heart problems, and instructed me to start some light aerobic exercise, along with a low-carb diet and no sugar. I tried the Xanax, but it made me feel spaced out so I only took it occasionally when the anxiety was too great.

I began to purchase and read books on anxiety to try to figure out what was going on which helped to a degree, but nothing gave me the answers I was looking for. I found myself at the local health food store and began to look for vitamins and supplements that could help me. There, I discovered Pantothenic Acid, or B5, which is sometimes referred to as the "anti-stress vitamin" because it may reverse some biological damage caused by stress. It turned out that Pantothenic Acid really helped me cope with stress, and I still take it today.

Over the next several months I battled anxiety on-and-off. What I really needed was rest, but that just didn't seem possible at that time. We were right in the middle of our renovation project for the new building, and I was juggling that along with my part time job at the mall, not to mention the ministry. Eventually, I developed chronic anxiety.

I would wake up in the morning and I could feel my heart thumping in my chest. When I would stand before the mirror to shave, my pulse was in the 90s. On church days my pulse was elevated further. I can remember sitting on the platform before I was going to preach and discreetly checking my pulse. Oftentimes, it would be over 100 beats per minute. After preaching, my pulse was usually around 120 and would stay there for up to six hours after the service! Of course, this was very concerning and I felt lousy.

I found a different doctor that prescribed Atenolol, a beta blocker which slows the heart and causes it to beat with less force, instead of Xanax. This didn't numb my mind and emotions like Xanax, nor was it addictive. I tried to use it only after I was finished preaching, unless I really needed some relief. Sunday, July 4th, 2004 we held our first church service in our newly renovated building. It was a great milestone for our church and very exciting. We now had a facility with plenty of parking and seating, but I had a difficult time enjoying it because of how I was feeling. How ironic that the building was being renovated, as I was falling apart. I myself needed some renovation.

During the first weekend of October 2004, our church hosted the ALJC Fall Conference and we dedicated our building to the Lord. Rev. Scotty Teets from New York was our guest speaker. Brother Teets formerly pastored in Jackson, Michigan and was my wife's Pastor when she was a teenager. He also performed our wedding ceremony in 1993. During that conference, Brother Teets and I bonded with each other and he became my mentor and ultimately one of the greatest influences in my life. He was a pastor's pastor and one of the most gifted men of God I have ever met. He encouraged me so many times during his life. He used to say to me, "Son, listen to an old man. I'm not going to be around always, so let me pour into your life." Whenever we talked on the phone he did most of the talking as I just listened. I wish I could have recorded those conversations because they were like seminars for a young preacher. I would get off the phone and feel ten feet tall. He functioned in the gifts of the Spirit. I can remember one day in particular he called me and said, "Scott, I was praying and I could feel your frustration." He then proceeded to read my mail, so to speak. One day as I was talking to him about my battles with stress he said, "You just need to eat a sandwich in another city." That was his way of saying you need to get away from things for a while and rest. I will forever love that man for his kindness, encouragement, and compassion, and the way he unselfishly poured into me those years we had together. After his passing I wrote a sympathy letter to Sister Teets and told her that when I get to Heaven, he will be one of the first people I look for.

The years 2005 through 2008 were like a wilderness to me. A wilderness is a place of numerous tests and trials, but also has many blessings and miracles. You are never without God in a wilderness season, but at times it may feel that way. During those three years I continued my on-and-off battle with anxiety. At times I felt that I was recovering, while at other times I felt myself slipping down again.

Here are two examples from my journal entries:

Journal entry 2/13/05:
"Thursday, especially, I felt like myself for the first time in years. I'm close to a full recovery."

Journal entry 2/17/05:
"I did it again. I put too much stress on myself and I'm once again struggling with anxiety. It's not, however, as bad as it used to be. I'm tired of this."

I would like to address the delicate balance between seeking God for healing versus finding help from doctors and medication. I've known some people that believe that Christians should never see a doctor or take medication, which in my opinion is a dangerous legalistic view. I knew of a single mother in her twenties that attended a church in our city that held this type of belief. I'm not going to disclose the denomination, nor judge, but I do want to share this story in hopes of helping someone else. This woman developed diabetes and instead of going to a doctor and getting a prescription for insulin she prayed to God for healing, which should be a Christian's first response to illness. However, she never saw a physician. God did not choose to heal her and she died at a young age, leaving three young and beautiful children without a mother. Had she gone to the doctor she could have most likely raised those children into adulthood, and may still be alive today.

The Old Testament tells the story of King Asa who became diseased in his feet, and stopped relying on God. *"Yet in his disease he sought not to the LORD, but to the physicians."* 2 Chronicles 16:12. This scripture is not telling us to be against doctors, or refuse to seek their help. It is simply telling us that he did not seek God for his healing.

I am fully persuaded that as Christians we should always go to God first for our healing. He is truly the Great Physician. However if healing does not come through prayer, it is not wrong to seek help from a doctor or take medication.

It's strange that sometimes we can pray for others when we are not feeling well, and they get healed, but we do not. One day, I prayed a total of seven hours for my healing after telling my wife how tired I was of what I was feeling. I intended to pray until I got my breakthrough. I prayed for five hours, took a short break to get a sandwich, and then prayed another two hours. While I was praying, my wife received a phone call from a lady who wanted us to pray for her mother who had been diagnosed with cancer. Later that evening we went to her mother's home. When we prayed for her the glory of God immediately filled the room and it was apparent that she received a touch from God. She went back to the doctor and soon received the report that the cancer was completely gone, yet my affliction continued.

Dr. Claire Weekes, in her book, *Hope and Help For Your Nerves*, states: "*Depression is a body's expression of emotional exhaustion.*" When a person has been battling stress and anxiety for a long time the body eventually becomes drained. It's like looking at life through smudged glasses. It's like trying to use a cell phone that needs to be recharged, or trying to start a vehicle that has a nearly dead battery. God in his mercy can jump-start us with a fresh anointing, but that does not disregard the need to rest and be recharged.

Throughout 2006, my Wilderness Journey continued, but the landscape gradually changed from gripping anxiety to dark depression, and crippling fatigue. In this same year, I chose to transfer my minister's license from the Assemblies of our Lord Jesus Christ to the United Pentecostal Church International. I did not leave the ALJC with any bad feelings or on bad terms, but for personal and pastoral reasons I felt led to make the change.

During this transition time I remember feeling constant tightness on the left side of my chest, in the same place where I had felt the initial pain from my panic attack in 2004. As I became more tired, the chest muscle would feel achy and tired. I went to several doctors to express my concerns and I had numerous EKGs, but every time it came back normal. This was a relief, but I still had that nagging tightness in the chest. I made an appointment with a Cardiologist and as I was sitting in the waiting room I looked at all the people who had real heart problems. Many of them could hardly walk or breathe. I sat there as a young man thinking, "What am I doing here?" When I spoke with the Cardiologist and explained my symptoms, he told me there was nothing wrong with my heart and basically told me that I needed to get out of his office.

Throughout 2007 and 2008 I battled debilitating fatigue. I would get up in the morning feeling wiped out, eat some breakfast and have some time of prayer, and then go back to bed. I wasn't tired enough to sleep, but I didn't have the energy to get up either, so I would just lay there. Trying to preach in those days was extremely difficult because I couldn't prepare sermons as in the past. My mind was too tired to prepare much in the way of notes, and my prayer life was dragging. I would lay on the floor prostrate until I felt God impress something on my heart, and that's what I would preach. Somehow God helped me through those years and I kept going, as did the church.

Many times I would start my messages by telling the church I wasn't feeling very well, but I would do the best that I could, which made people ask my wife if I was okay. She told me it might be best if I never mentioned how I was feeling, but just get up there and preach. When I started doing that, people stopped asking about my condition. Apparently they couldn't tell that I was struggling. God has a way of using us, even in our weakness.

I was also still working my part time job at the mall, which was equally difficult because it required that I be on my feet all day. I can remember one day I was walking down the mall when a total stranger looked at me and said, "Man, you look like one tired guy." I looked back at him with my brain fog, expressionless, thinking --- "Thanks a lot pal."

Another day I was walking to my car after finishing my shift, and I had to stop halfway through the parking lot because I really didn't know if I would make it to my car. I can't explain how tired I felt. I simply had no energy, and I still had that nagging tension and tiredness in my chest. At times, it truly felt like I was dying.

On December 5th, 2008, I went into prayer desperate for a touch from God. I was very careful to choose words that I thought would be pleasing to the Lord and to show reverence, but for some reason the Lord seemed distant. In fact, I couldn't feel the presence of God at all. I tried everything from repenting, to worshiping, to giving thanks, to quoting scripture. When I finished praying I felt disappointed and got up and sat in a chair and sighed. As I sighed, the Holy Ghost spoke these beautiful words: "*You don't have to perform for me, I will perform for you.*" What a paradigm shift in thinking. Those few words were life-changing to me! They made me feel so loved and accepted by God. I no longer felt like I needed to impress Him. Until that time I had never realized that I was trying to perform for Him. Reflecting back, I realized that I subconsciously was trying to earn his love and acceptance, which is something none of us ever have to do: by nature, God can't help but love us. The scripture tells us that God is love.

"He that loveth not knoweth not God; for God is love."
1 John 4:8

*"Being confident of this very thing,
he which hath begun a good work in you
will perform it until the day of Jesus Christ."*
Philippians 1:6

Later in December of 2008, I experienced another ray of hope when I visited a doctor in East Lansing. He suspected I was suffering from low testosterone, so he ordered some lab work. According to WebMD.com[2], the normal total testosterone levels for a man are 300 to 1,000 ng/dl, but my total testosterone level was 166.

---

2) https://www.webmd.com/men/features/keep-testosterone-in-balance

I didn't even make the bottom rung of the ladder, so no wonder I felt wiped out. I had a nurse tell me that stress burns through hormones, and I realized that all of the stress I had allowed myself to carry made me deficient in this area. Sometimes it can be a relief just to know what is wrong with you!

The doctor suggested that I start testosterone replacement therapy. He prescribed a cream that I would apply daily to my upper arm or the back of my neck. I could immediately feel the difference in energy, but I have to confess I never felt completely normal while using the cream.

It was always hard for me to find a sweet spot, in terms of the perfect amount that my body needed. Hormones are extremely powerful. When mine were not balanced correctly, I really battled things in my mind and emotions. There are pros and cons to testosterone replacement therapy. The good news is that it does give your body what it is lacking. The bad news is, once a man starts using testosterone he will most likely be on it for the rest of his life.

This is because when supplemental doses are introduced, then the brain thinks the body doesn't need to produce it any longer, or at least not as much as before. I've even heard stories of men that have tried to stop using testosterone and went through long withdrawal periods that were absolutely agonizing, so they had no choice but to go back to using the testosterone medication.

In retrospect, I would have not started using testosterone right away. Instead, I would have searched for other ways to raise my testosterone naturally. There are many different herbs and other supplements that can help. Each person needs to do their own research and make the best choice for themselves alongside their physician, taking into account any and all other medical conditions.

When I started testosterone therapy I really felt like I had found the key to my healing. I had read stories of how other men with testosterone deficiency felt brand new once starting testosterone replacement therapy. I was so encouraged and ready to be over all of this struggle. It was time to close an old chapter in my life and begin a new one. In my mind I felt like it was time for my comeback to occur. In 2021, I abandoned the testosterone cream and started giving myself weekly injections, which for me has been much better. I'll discuss that later in the book. Nevertheless, testosterone replacement therapy was a game-changer for me.

CHAPTER FOUR
MY COMEBACK

*"Rejoice not against me, O mine enemy:
when I fall, I shall arise; when I sit in darkness,
the LORD shall be a light unto me."*
Micah 7:8

In order to have a comeback, a person has to have something to come back from. The children of Israel "came back" from Egyptian bondage, Elijah the prophet "came back" from the cave, the three Hebrews "came back" from the fiery furnace, Daniel "came back" from the Lion's Den, Jonah "came back" from the fish's belly, Lazarus "came back" from the grave, Thomas "came back" after doubting Jesus Christ, and Simon Peter "came back" after denying Jesus Christ.

Considering my own afflictions that I experienced for over 20 years, I had plenty to come back from. As I write this I can't help but feel in my spirit that somebody reading these words needs a comeback. Perhaps you have suffered a season of confusion. You have prayed and believed in God, but the answers have not come. Trust me when I tell you it's not time to give up, but instead it's time to be strong, to put on the whole armor of God, and to press on. We serve a God who delights in helping people come back from adversity and pain. Sickness, setbacks and attacks of the enemy are fertile soil for God to give you a comeback. The psalmist said that weeping may endure for a night. We must understand that he didn't say how long the night would last, but we must trust that the night will eventually end, and joy will come in the morning. As Job 28:3 declares, "*He setteth end to the darkness.*"

When I think of the term "*comeback*", I think of recovery and restoration, returning to a former position or condition, or the return of health and vitality. To me it means rising up out of the ashes to stand victorious again, overcoming mountainous obstacles. When you experience a comeback means that your test has now become your testimony.

My comeback was not instantaneous, but gradual. "*The steps of a good man are ordered by the LORD: and He delighteth in his way.*" Psalm 37:23. Step-by-step, little by little, the Lord started leading me back to a place of well-being and greater effectiveness in life and ministry. I wished it would have happened overnight, and I have to confess there were times I became impatient with God's slow process. Through this, however, I have learned that God is not only slow to anger, but He can also be slow in unfolding His purpose in our lives. Even as I write this, I am still in the process of making a complete comeback. God, however, knows what He's doing with each of us, and He never makes a mistake. Even our suffering is in the plan of God which many times will include valleys, storms, fiery trials, divers temptations, and disappointments. Come what may, we must remember that we serve a sovereign God that loves us completely, and is too powerful and omniscient to make a mistake. God is not in the business of making mistakes—He is in the business of making disciples.

When I started using testosterone cream, I had high hopes that it was the answer to my health battles. This made perfect sense because the lab work showed that my testosterone levels were so deficient. I thought for sure that my comeback was imminent, but I soon found out that things were not going to be quite that simple for me. My wife has always joked through the years saying that I'm a complicated man, and she's right. When I started the testosterone therapy I felt an increase of energy, but I could never get my testosterone levels to rise past 400 or 500 ng/dl. Remember, the experts agree that normal total testosterone levels for a man range from 300 to 1,000 ng/dl[1].

When I tried to increase my dose, I found that I was very sensitive to testosterone. If I took too much, I would either feel aggressive or my mind would feel *snowy*.

1) https://www.webmd.com/men/features/keep-testosterone-in-balance

When I say snowy, think of driving down a back country road in Michigan during a snowstorm. Snow can be hypnotic; you have to stay focused and drive slowly, so you don't end up in the ditch. That's what my mind felt like when I had too much testosterone. My thoughts were sluggish and I had to focus when trying to navigate a simple conversation with people.

If I took too little testosterone, I felt myself dragging. Of course, I thought of giving up the testosterone completely, but then I would go back to debilitating fatigue, which was not an option. I've often said that trying to find the right dose for me was like trying to catch a wild rabbit: nearly impossible. Some men do very well on testosterone cream and have no troubles to speak of. Unfortunately, I was not one of them. Thus my love-hate relationship with testosterone began.

While it's true that the testosterone therapy improved my overall energy, I was still battling fatigue… It just wasn't as severe as before. I began to realize that my health battles went much deeper than just a testosterone issue. There were obviously other things at play, but I had no idea what those things were.

During the years of 2008 and 2009 my wilderness journey continued. The days of chronic anxiety seemed well behind me, yet occasionally it would raise its ugly head. When Jesus finished His wilderness temptation the Bible said the devil departed from Him for a season, which meant that the devil did come back from time to time. This is what my anxiety was like, but I have learned that once you defeat something it can never dominate you to the same degree as in the past. Perhaps that's one of the reasons God lets us go through our struggles. They teach us wisdom, knowledge, warfare skills, and how to meditate, think, and handle things.

> "He that handleth a matter wisely shall find good."
> Proverbs 16:20

On September 9th, 2009 I suffered a severe case of appendicitis and had to have an appendectomy. The doctor said my appendix was crystallized and nearly at the point of bursting. I was very sick. Two days later I was released from the hospital and grateful to be home, but I had a very difficult time recovering. Here is one of my journal entries:

Journal entry 9/19/09:
Today was the lowest day I've had in months. I felt unmotivated, lifeless, and depressed all day. Marissa and Debbie wanted to look at a house that was for sale. I came away feeling stress in my chest. I felt fear and depression. I suffered in my mind. The thought came to me— "You will have to give up the ministry, file bankruptcy and live out

your existence." I came home and wept. I talked with Debbie and she suggested that I talk to the Lord. As soon as she left the room I began to pour out my heart to him and strong tongues flowed out of me. I could feel the light shining in the darkness. I asked the Lord to give me a word concerning the future of my ministry; something to anchor my soul in. Immediately the thought came to me, "The gifts and calling of God are without repentance."

Of course I realized that those words were in the Bible, but when I felt the Lord speak them to me they had such a profound effect. It was as if He was saying it didn't matter the condition of my mind, my emotions, or my body - His gifts will still flow through me and He will never take away my calling. Immediately I felt in my spirit that I was going to be okay. The Lord had spoken and Satan was defeated.

A few days later it felt like I had the flu and I was running a fever. When I went back to the doctor it was discovered that I had an E. coli infection from the surgery, which meant that I had to go back to the hospital to have my stomach drained. I felt so terrible during that time that I remember not reading my Bible, except for one verse each day. I would open the Bible up in the morning and read the first verse of scripture I saw. I did this for three days and every day the scripture I read was exactly what I needed for the day. I still remember the three scriptures that the Lord gave me.

Day 1: "For He remembered His holy promise, and Abraham His servant." Psalm 105:42. I inserted my name in place of Abraham's. It encouraged me to realize that God was remembering his promises to me.

Day 2: The righteous shall be glad in the LORD, And shall trust in Him; and all the upright in heart shall glory. " Psalm 64:10. After reading this scripture I was wheeled down the hospital hallway for a CT scan, where a thin plastic tube would be inserted in my stomach to drain the infection. I was left sitting in the hallway alone and was given one of those warm blankets. In my opinion, warm blankets are the best part of being in the hospital. While I was waiting, I felt the sweet presence of the Holy Ghost come all over me and the joy of the Lord sprang up in my spirit. I began to laugh with joy and briefly spoke with tongues. That was a special anointing that day. In my 28 years of being filled with the Holy Ghost I have never felt that kind of joy before, nor since. Maybe this is what Isaiah meant when he spoke of *"the oil of joy for mourning."* Maybe this is what Jesus meant when he told the Apostle Paul," *My grace is sufficient for thee: for my strength is made perfect in weakness."*

Day 3: "And when the Lord saw her, He had compassion on her, And said unto her, Weep not." Luke 7:13. The scripture let me know that the Lord saw me, had compassion on me, and did not want me to weep.

After I got out of the hospital the first church service I went to there was a message in tongues and interpretation: *"Yea, I see you in suffering and I know your brokenness. Come with me. I will go before you and make the crooked places straight. Trust in me."*

At the beginning of 2010 we were trying to purchase the building we were having church in. Up until that time we had been leasing it, but we were having trouble getting a loan and had just been denied again on February 6th. My brother-in-law was the owner of the building and was wanting to sell it to us. He was extremely patient and gracious but he had other offers, so when we had trouble getting those loans it created a lot of pressure for me.

On Sunday evening, March 14th, 2010 I received a call from David Clary from Louisiana. He and I are the type of long-time friends that can go six months or longer without speaking, and pick things right up as if we had just spoken the day before. On that day, he told me the most amazing thing: he had just received a card in the mail that he had attempted to send to us two and a half years prior. It was meant to encourage us in our ministry and building project. On the envelope it was stamped "*Return to Sender*". When he placed it on his kitchen table he said, "I don't believe in coincidence." He felt there was a reason why that card had been lost in the mail, and at that point the Lord began to speak to him. The Lord told him that I was struggling and was questioning my ministry. The Lord told him that just like that card was delayed, but not denied; so my blessings were being delayed, but not denied. So he placed it back in the mail the next week and sent it back to us. This was amazing to me because Brother Clary and I had not spoken in months. He had no idea what was going on with me, but God did.

Journal entry: 3/14/10
Today Brother Clary preached to his church - "Delayed, but not Denied." Throughout the message he made reference to me. He felt as though it was a word for me and our church. He told me: " You're under spiritual opposition, hold on, don't question your ministry, don't give up, don't lose hope."

Two days later I called in sick, due to exhaustion. I received a phone call from Brother Victor Rodriguez, who has since passed, and was one of the most faithful members of my church. He told me his wife was praying for me the night before, and had a vision of a large green tree that was having its branches cut off. She was living in Texas at the time, and had no idea what I was going through, except the Lord had spoken to her.

This made me think of how King Nebuchadnezzar saw himself as a large tree that was cut down, and left with just the stump of his roots in the earth, but afterward he said: "*I was established in my kingdom, and excellent majesty was added unto me."* I remember Brother Jeff Arnold spoke once about how sometimes God allows affliction in your life and you're left with just a stump, but through the scent of water you can bud and bring forth fruit again. I can see now that God was anchoring my faith and giving me hope. I was not being destroyed, but developed. Fruit was in my future, but I just couldn't see it. On Monday, August 9th, 2010 I attended a revival service at Brother David Trammell's church, where Brother Doug Klinedinst was preaching.

Journal entry: 8/9/10
Brother Doug Klinedinst prophesied over me tonight; I'm coming into a new season. It's time to deny myself; pick up my cross; and consecrate myself. God is going to give me revelation. The heavens will be rolled back. I will see things I've never seen. I will be stronger in doctrine.

The next evening I attended the revival again, and I asked Brother Klinedinst to pray over me at the altar. I told him of my health battles, and I told him that I felt like my testosterone levels were hindering my ministry. He told me that my testosterone levels were not affecting my ministry like I thought, but that the enemy likes to magnify our shortcomings to discourage us. He prayed against the attacks of the enemy, and prophesied healing to me. He said that with every breath I took I would become stronger. Time has proven that to be true.

On December 31st, 2010, I received a call from our bank that we were approved for our church loan. What a great way to end the year! It was a great feeling to announce the news to our church at the next Sunday service. The building was now ours and the feelings of uncertainty were lifted from our minds. At least I could say that one thing was settled in my life. Truly the blessings had been delayed, but not denied.

I had come through an abundance of afflictions and the Lord had been very good to me, but unfortunately the years 2011 through 2013 proved not to be any easier for me health-wise. I continued to use the testosterone cream, which helped, but I still battled fatigue most of the time and often my mind was still sluggish. I had no stamina. I knew there had to be something else going on with me, but I couldn't figure out what it was. None of the doctors I had gone to had any answers for me, and the Lord seemed to be quiet. So I just kept living for God and preaching the gospel. I heard one preacher say that if you can't change your situation, just outlive it. That's what I planned on doing. Psalms 37:3 declares, "Trust in the LORD, and do good." God had spoken enough to me in the past few months and years that I had no doubt he was with me. I knew that no matter what happened, my ministry was secure and God was with me. I felt anchored.

In spite of the fact that my health was not improving like I wanted, I don't believe those were wasted years. I believe that even when we struggle, God has a purpose. It's during times like that that we can learn and grow, discovering things about ourselves, the people around us, and the God that we worship and serve. I look back at those years and view them as discovery years.

"And thou shalt remember all the way which the Lord thy God led thee these forty years in the wilderness, to humble thee, and to prove thee, to know what was in thine heart, whether thou wouldest keep his commandments, or no. And he humbled thee, and suffered thee to hunger, and fed thee with manna, which thou knewest not, neither did thy fathers know; that he might make thee know that man doth not live by bread only, but by every word that proceedeth out of the mouth of the Lord doth man live."
Deuteronomy 8:2-3

At 91 years old, Pastor Andrews left this earth to be with the Lord on December 12th, 2013. I was privileged to preach at his funeral, where the Lord gave me a message from Genesis 48:21: Jacob said to Joseph, *"Behold, I die: but God shall be with you."* It was a very emotional service because people loved that precious man so much. He had a genuine love for people and they genuinely loved him in return. Sometimes we don't realize how much people have touched our lives until they're actually gone, and after he passed I began to feel a void in my life. I suddenly realized that I had no man of God to speak into my life and felt very uncomfortable with that. Brother Teets was still living, but he was also battling some health issues and was no longer able to minister to me as before. Hence, I began to pray that God would send a pastor into my life. Every Christian needs a pastor. Even the pastor himself needs a pastor. We are all in spiritual warfare and we need someone that we can be accountable to. We need someone that can counsel us and give us guidance in times of need. We need someone we can look to for wisdom and strength. Having a pastor is a safeguard in our lives, because we all have blind spots and sometimes we can't see our own deficiencies. At other times we simply need someone we can open our hearts to; someone that can offer encouragement when we are down. God answered my prayers very quickly.

It happened in 2014 at our Michigan District camp meeting. I was standing at the book table speaking with Bishop Keith McKinnies and we both felt a divine connection. I had known Bishop McKinnies since 2006 when I had gone before the board for my minister's license, but up until that time we had been just acquaintances. However on that day, something clicked between the two of us. He would later tell me that he'd actually had our church in Jackson in his heart, and that he had been praying for us! We both believe that God put us together.

We soon arranged to have lunch together and he offered to drive from Flint to Jackson to meet me. We had a good time getting to know each other and I opened up to him about my health battles. He told me that he had once preached a message about Daniel in the lion's den entitled, *"Sometimes We Have to Live With Our Lions"*. That was encouraging to me because it made me realize that sometimes God allows us to go through things that we don't like, yet he allows them for a season to develop us, and our relationship with him. The struggles of life also allow us to be a witness to other people. Our testimony of what God has done for us is our greatest witness. Our testimony is also our greatest source of encouragement when the enemy fights us. We can look back at what God has done and know that if God did *that* – then God can do *this*.

"David said moreover, The Lord that delivered me out of the paw of the lion, and out of the paw of the bear, he will deliver me out of the hand of this Philistine. And Saul said unto David, Go, and the Lord be with thee."
1 Samuel 17:37

Bishop McKinnies preached his first sermon to our church November 2nd, 2014. That day it became apparent to me why God had yoked us together. Bishop McKinnies and I are similar in many ways, yet different in others. I was so impressed with his easy approach to the ministry of the word. He had such a calm demeanor. He didn't seem to be struggling or forcing the message. He was enjoying himself and letting God use him. This is something I desperately needed to see modeled before my eyes. I never realized how much I had pushed myself to preach the word of God to try to be the perfect preacher. I had a doctor one time tell me that perfectionism comes off in layers. I truly believe that God sent Bishop McKinnies to help peel back the layers of perfectionism that had bound me for so long. This was essential if I was going to find healing in my life. Looking back, I realize that much of my stress has been self-induced because of perfectionism and the mentality of pushing myself and putting more on myself than God ever meant for me to carry. I've learned through the school of hard knocks that God actually wants us as ministers to enjoy our calling. Do yourself a favor sometime and look up all the scriptures where the Lord talks about how he wants us to be full of joy. I don't believe God has ever called a man into the ministry to make him miserable. In the presence of the Lord there is a fullness of joy. Salvation and joy are supposed to go together. Bishop McKinnies has since preached at our church nearly every month during the last seven years. As I am writing this book he has preached over 70 messages to our church. I consider him not only my pastor and mentor, but one of my very best friends. It is truly an honor to have him in my life.

*"Thou wilt shew me the path of life:
in thy presence is fulness of joy;
at thy right hand there are pleasures for evermore."*
Psalm 16:11

In January of 2015 I learned of the Born Clinic located in Grand Rapids, Michigan, which is a leading clinic in preventive medicine. They combine the best emerging practices with tried-and-tested techniques of conventional medicine to uncover the root causes of a patient's symptoms. After my first visit I was very encouraged. The doctor that I saw told me that many of his patients are ministers or minister's wives that are stressed out due to the ministry. Hearing that made me feel right at home. One of the tests that they performed on me was a food sensitivity test. From a blood sample they were able to determine that I was sensitive to several different foods. I also tested positive for candidiasis, which is a fungal infection caused by yeast. Candida is the scientific name for yeast, a fungus that lives almost everywhere, including inside your body. Usually, your immune system keeps yeast under control. If you are sick or taking antibiotics, it can multiply and cause an infection. However, it can also stem from ongoing stress, which was probably what had happened to me. Unfortunately, I had a candida overgrowth in my gut.

There are basically three ways to fight candida. Number one is to take an anti-fungal drug. Number two is to go on a

Candida Diet. Number three is a combination of those two. I chose to avoid the anti-fungal drug, and opted for the diet alone. A Candida Diet means that you have to eliminate foods that are feeding the candida in your stomach. Candida is a living organism and it thrives on sugar and yeast products. If you stop feeding it it will eventually die off, but the whole process is not as easy as it sounds. Interestingly, the foods that I was sensitive to were mostly the foods that were feeding my candida. In other words, the food I was eating was making and keeping me sick.

As Christians we may think that we can eat anything that we want and still live a healthy life, but that is far from the truth. I remember one time hearing a Christian comedian on the radio. He joked about how Christians, before eating an unhealthy snack like a Twinkie, would pray over it and say, "Lord, please bless this Twinkie and as it goes down my esophagus, change its molecular structure so that it is loaded with nutrients and minerals to nourish my body in Jesus' name." That is obviously ridiculous, but it's what so many of us do everyday. We cannot eat junk food continuously and then hope to live a healthy life.

The Candida Diet that I was placed on was scheduled to last for 90 days. My doctor said that many of his patients, however, choose to continue eating this way for the rest of their lives. When I started that diet I learned the powerful addiction of sugar. If you've never had sugar withdrawal symptoms, believe me you don't want to experience them. Sugar withdrawal symptoms can include an intense craving for something sweet, irritability, a depressed mood, and flu-like symptoms. Before starting the diet, I was literally addicted to Chips Ahoy chocolate chip cookies. I always had to have them in the house. I would grab a cookie on the way out of the house. I would grab one walking through the kitchen. I would take a couple to church and eat them in my office before I preached. I would maybe have one or two before bedtime. Who has ever heard of a chocolate chip cookie addict? Sure enough, soon after giving up chocolate chip cookies and other types of sugar I found myself intensely craving sweets, irritable, and feeling like I had a mild case of the flu. I remember walking in church one Sunday morning and one of the ladies said — "You look like you don't feel well at all." Sugar withdrawals last from a few days to a couple of weeks, depending on the individual, but things do get better. Once your body has detoxed you begin to feel clearer thinking and a better sense of well-being.

When I started the Candida Diet, I weighed 184 pounds. After following the diet for 90 days, I was down to 158. The brain fog was gone and I was feeling better overall. I wasn't 100% and I was still battling fatigue, but it was definitely a step in the right direction. Don't worry - I did eventually gain most of that weight back.

Throughout my journey I have also learned other lessons such as the importance of getting some moderate exercise, such as walking. I say *moderate* because when your body is worn out and you're trying to rebuild, too much exercise can be just as bad as no exercise at all. I try to walk at least three times a week just to keep the blood flowing. *"The life of the flesh is in the blood..."* (Leviticus 17:11). We've got to keep that blood flowing. Getting proper rest is also important. As one doctor said, sleep is a stress-buster. There's a lot of healing that takes place in our bodies when we sleep. Psalm 127:2 says, *"He giveth his beloved sleep."* Sleep is a gift from God. It's part of how we have been fearfully and wonderfully made. David said, *"I laid me down and slept; I awaked; for the LORD sustained me."* Psalm 3:5. On the contrary, when we are sleep deprived we feel grumpy, which is our body's way of saying, *"Hey, you're messing up God's plan!"* I believe God has a lot of ways of speaking to us, but sometimes we don't listen, or we may not recognize that He's trying to communicate with us.

Proper vitamins and supplements can also be highly beneficial, especially if our body is in a depleted state. Everyday I take multi minerals, Magnesium, Vitamin C, B Complex, and Pantothenic Acid. In the wintertime I'll take Vitamin D because we don't get as much sunlight during those months, and I try to add some Zinc to boost my immune system during the cold and flu season. Adaptogens are also an awesome way to help with stress-related fatigue.

Research shows that adaptogens can combat fatigue, enhance mental performance, and help ease depression and anxiety. Adaptogens help us to *adapt* to stress.[1] A list of adaptogens would include Asian Ginseng, Rhodiola, Cordyceps and Ashwagandha, just to name a few. For adrenal fatigue, I take a product called Adrenal Rebuilder made by Doctor James L. Wilson. You can find his products at adrenalfatigue.org. This product has worked wonders for me over the years and has pulled me out of the pit of adrenal fatigue more than once.

I would highly recommend looking into the supplements listed above if a reader relates to my story and symptoms, but I first advise a consultation with a physician before taking anything new. This is not medical advice, and a person should do their own research and consult with their medical professional before putting anything into their body. There are risks to introducing new things into your body if it does not really need it, and a new supplement could interact with current medication, possibly causing adverse effects.

Adrenal glands release stress hormones into our body when we are under stress, such as adrenaline and cortisol. When we have been under stress for a long time, the adrenal glands can actually become depleted and weak.

1) *https://www.healthline.com/health/stress/smart-girls-guide-to-adaptogens*

That's why high cortisol levels eventually lead to a crash. This causes fatigue and the adrenal glands need to be restored. Sometimes when people are suffering from tired adrenal glands, they will start reaching for that extra cup of coffee to get a caffeine boost. This may help us for a while, but it's like putting a Band-Aid on a much bigger problem. As Christians we know that God is in the restoration business, but sometimes he needs us to rest in order for that restoration to manifest. In Psalm 23, David said, *"He maketh me lie down in green pastures, he leadeth me beside the still waters."* God doesn't lead us all the time. Sometimes he wants us to lie down, but as Christians we like to run all the time. We sometimes feel pressured because we know we're living in the last days and we feel like we've got to get it all done now, but the word of God still says, *"be still and know that I am God."* If you and I need to take the time to rest, I'm convinced that God can run His universe and His church just fine without our help. In fact, we would probably be a lot more efficient and fruitful if we would learn to rest more often instead of waiting until we're absolutely worn out and then go crawling into God's presence and asking God to please heal us. Don't forget that Jesus said, *"I am the vine and you are the branches."* I have never seen a branch strain, struggle or break out in a sweat trying to produce fruit. The only thing the branch has to do in order to be fruitful is stay attached to the vine. Life and power is in the vine.

After following the Candida Diet for 90 days as instructed, I was able to gradually reintroduce some foods back into my diet. However, I was advised to stay away from some foods for the rest of my life, such as: brewer's yeast, baker's yeast, gluten, and anything high in sugar. This was hard for me because I enjoyed breads, pizzas, hamburgers, and coney dogs; not to mention ice cream in the summer and cheesecake anytime. Therefore I have since had to find a place of moderation, which I think holds true for so many other facets of life as well. Most of the time I still eat healthy, but once in a while… well, let's not talk about that. Overall I would say that the diet helped, but I was still not feeling like myself. I felt like I had reached a plateau. The testosterone replacement therapy had helped, the Candida Diet had helped, but I still felt that something was missing. I had good days and bad days. There were times I felt very strong in prayer and in preaching, while other times it seemed like a struggle to do the basic things required in the ministry.

A few times I tried to confide with certain people in the church about how I was feeling, but they couldn't grasp what I was saying. According to them I looked fine and there seemed to be no hindrance in my ministry. I began to realize that there was no way people could tell how I was feeling just by looking at me because when I tried to explain it to them they still didn't understand it. To be honest, I didn't even understand it myself. I would see people in public that I hadn't seen for months or years and they would remark how good I looked. I remember one time going to a doctor for a physical and he said that it was nice to actually see a healthy patient.

In August of 2015, the Lord gave me a message to preach at Bishop McKinnies' church that I will never forget. It was entitled, "*If You Will Carry the Presence of the Lord, the Presence of the Lord Will Carry you.*" I will share the nuts and bolts of that message because I think it will help somebody. In fact, I have since preached it twice in my church.

Psalm 68:1 says, "*Let God arise, and his enemies be scattered: let them also that hate him flee before him.*" This was a Psalm of David, but it was first a prayer of Moses. Numbers 10:35 says, "*And it came to pass, when the ark set forward, that Moses said, rise up, LORD, and let thine enemies be scattered; and let them that hate thee flee before them*". The ark is a symbol of God's presence, so this was a picture of the Israelites carrying the presence of God. As New Testament believers, we literally carry the presence of God when we are filled with the Holy Ghost.

Psalm 68:19 says, "*Blessed **be** the Lord, **who** daily loadeth us **with benefits, even** the God of our salvation. Selah.*" When you read this scripture in the King James version, the words that I highlighted are in italics. This means they were added by the King James translators and were not in the original Hebrew text. The translators would add words in order for the scriptures to make sense in our English language. If you take those words out of Psalms 68:19 it would say, "*Blessed the Lord, daily loadeth us, the God of our salvation. Selah.*"

The word loadeth in Hebrew means to load, be borne, or carry a load. Adam Clarke's commentary says, "*It would be better to translate the clause thus: 'Blessed be the Lord, who supports us day by day.'*" He said the word loadeth means to lift, bear up, support, or to bear a burden for another. In full, Clarke said that Psalm 68:19 could be translated, "*Blessed be the Lord day by day, who bears our burdens for us.*" This means that the Lord carries us day by day!

Isaiah 46:3-5 declares, "*Hearken unto me, O house of Jacob, and all the remnant of the house of Israel, which are borne by me from the belly, which are carried from the womb. And even to your old age I am he; and even to hoar hairs will I carry you: I have made, and I will bear; even I will carry, and deliver you.*"

If you pause and look back over your own life, I'm sure you can reflect on specific times when the Lord carried you. Maybe you were empty or weak because of the load you had been carrying, but somehow you felt the hand of God lift you up, giving you the strength to go on. Those in leadership know exactly what it is to be drained. I'm not just speaking of pastors and their wives, but a leader can be a mother or a father, or a grandparent, or even a young person that's had to step up to the plate and be mature before adulthood. Responsibility of any kind can get heavy, and it is so good to know that we can lay it all at the Master's feet, lift up our hands, and let Him carry us. Truly, they that wait upon the Lord shall renew their strength.

In 2016 my mother-in-law, Petra Andrews, became very ill. She had been battling heart disease and was now on dialysis several times a week for kidney failure. My father-in-law was her caretaker and took her to all of her appointments. My wife had always been very close to her parents and during that time made sure to call them every day. Many times we prayed for my mother-in-law over the phone, and sometimes in person. On October 13th, 2016, Petra passed away. That was a tough time for our family, especially my wife, but the Lord carried us. I preached at my mother-in-law's funeral, which was one of the hardest things I have ever done. We loved her dearly, but we knew that she was in the presence of the Lord. She always had a strong faith in God and was not ashamed to share her testimony. Suddenly my wife and I found that we were without one of our parents and it seemed very strange. It's not realistic, but you always feel like your parents will be there forever.

Also in 2016, I encountered a new health battle. As summer was coming to a close I began to have a nagging kink in my neck. If you remember in the beginning of this book I mentioned I had first gone to a chiropractor that helped me to heal from tendonitis in both of my arms. Afterward, I continued to see the same chiropractor about once per month. Suddenly, however, I found myself going at least once a week, but it wasn't working. It progressed to a dull toothache-like pain in both of my shoulders. It got so bad that I couldn't sleep at night and would literally wake up three times a night to ice my shoulders. I could barely raise my arms over my head. I had to stand on my tiptoes to reach for cups, bowls or dishes in the cupboard. My wife would have to help me get dressed because I couldn't get a shirt on over my head. It was almost impossible to comb my hair. I stand 5' 10" tall. I put a mark on the wall of how high I could reach, which was only 5" above my head. My shoulders were locked up! My Chiropractor did everything he knew to help me, but it was to no avail.

I started seeing an Osteopath in Grand Rapids who was esteemed as the number one pain specialist in Michigan. He had high hopes of helping me, but everything he tried failed. Besides adjustments, he tried prolotherapy injections, which entailed 4-5 shots in each shoulder all during one visit. I felt like a pin cushion. When that didn't work he tried cortisone injections, but they also failed. Over the course of two months, I spent at least $2,000 and instead of getting better, I grew worse. I humorously felt like the woman with the issue of blood. If only I could have touched the hem of Jesus' garment!

One day while searching the internet for answers I learned of a condition called frozen shoulder. From there I learned of a doctor in Brighton, Michigan, who claimed to have a special therapy that was tried and proven to work. I visited his office for a free examination and he told me that he could help me. He said he would have to see me Monday through Friday, 5 straight days, and that it would cost me $7,000. He wanted the money up front. I told him that was a lot of money, and asked if there was any type of a money back guarantee, which there was not. Needless to say, that was my last visit to his office.

At this point I had suffered for three long months. I was achy all of the time and sleep deprived. One of the men in my church told me about his chiropractor that resides in my hometown of Jackson. He said that he had seen people carried into his chiropractor's office and then walk out under their own power. At this point I was skeptical but desperate for any help I could get. As it turned out he was able to help me, but it would cost me a great deal. He wanted to put me on a program that would last for several months and it would cost me about $5,000. I didn't have that kind of money, but this man at my church told me if I would go for the treatments, that he would pay for them out of his own pocket. What a blessing that was! This was another example of how God carries us when we can't carry ourselves.

After about six months of treatments, I was able to fully raise my arms over my head, sleep through the night, and dress myself. I had a new reason to lift my hands in praise to God. Many times I felt amazed at the way God brought me through that trial, but while I was rejoicing… a storm was brewing.

> *"Lift up your hands in the sanctuary,*
> *and bless the LORD."*
> Psalm 134:2

CHAPTER FIVE
MY CHALLENGES

"And he said unto Abram, know of a surety that thy seed shall be a stranger in a land that is not theirs, and shall serve them; and they shall afflict them four hundred years; And also that nation, whom they shall serve, will I judge: and afterward shall they come out with great substance."
Genesis 15:13-14

I entered 2017 feeling discouraged because we had lost several families in our church, and our attendance was down. Bishop McKinnies has often told me that when the church is doing good the pastor feels good, but when the church is down then the pastor feels down. I learned firsthand that it is hard for a pastor to separate himself from his church. Many, many years ago someone asked the late Bishop Don Johnson the question, "Why don't you just take a vacation and get away from it all?" His response was, "There's not much in the way of a vacation because the church is on your mind all the time." How true that is.

I scheduled to have lunch with Bishop McKinnies to talk about how I was feeling, and to plan out some strategies for the new year. Bear in mind I was still battling fatigue, and still using testosterone cream therapy. Despite being on testosterone for several years, my testosterone levels were still not very good, which caused moments of discouragement and often a lack of motivation. One of the greatest struggles for me was to have a desire to pray, study, and minister, and yet not feel good enough to do what was in my heart. Bishop McKinnies was such a great encouragement to me. He told me that I was a good pastor and had a good church. He suggested that I should keep doing what I was doing, but maybe add a few special services. I then contacted Brother Clary and scheduled a three-day revival for the spring. On the first night of that very revival, Brother Clary preached a message called, "Don't Settle for Less Than Your Dream." Throughout that message he encouraged our church to go back to dreaming again; to believe God for big things and not give up on our vision. What a wonderful message that was, and perfectly timed!

After the revival ended I decided to just do what I could do, and leave the rest to God. After all, it was God's church, not mine. My role was that of a grateful and privileged servant. I would pray and then preach whatever God gave me. I started to relax in my mind and believe that I had good seed, and that good ground was out there. I remember many years ago hearing Bishop Richard Curton preach about how the church has good seed. He talked about being a young man and living on the farm with his father. He reminisced about how farmers would sit around during the winter months and dream about the harvest of the coming season. They dreamed about what would happen if they got out there in the field and sowed their seed. I took that type of attitude into the rest of the year. I simply went to church and sowed whatever seed God gave me. I started to relax even with my negative body symptoms. I also started doing quite a bit of expository teaching, which for me comes very natural and easy. I love how you can teach the word of God and without exerting yourself or raising your voice, the Holy Ghost will move. Before I knew it, I could sense the church coming back to life, or maybe it was just me coming back to life. I have learned that if I will just preach what God gives me and not overly exert myself, the anointing of God will flow. Don't misunderstand me, I love to raise my voice and get loud when I preach. I don't know how anyone could feel the Holy Ghost and not become expressive in that manner. However it is worth recognizing that some of the preaching today is just noise without the anointing. If a man will preach what God gives him, God will confirm his preaching with an anointing.

By the end of 2017, we began to have visitors coming to the church and several stayed. Through a long season of God's sovereign work, thirteen total were baptized in Jesus' name and fourteen received the baptism of the Holy Ghost! On top of that, there was a great revival spirit in the church. The saints were being renewed and every service was full of expectation that God was doing something new.

However as life would have it, in the midst of experiencing this revival I received bad news. We had been having trouble with the boiler in our church for several months, and many different contractors had tried to get it up and running to no avail. Finally, on January 16th, 2018, the boiler was shut down indefinitely. Upon receiving that news, my heart sank. How would we come up with the money to get a new heating system? Where would we have church in the interim? Was there a way we could still hold church services in our building?

My first concern was the infrastructure temperature. It was about ten degrees outside, so I needed to find a way to keep the pipes from freezing. I called several of our church members and gathered all the space heaters I could find. We placed them strategically throughout the building, not knowing if it would work, but thankfully it did. My next concern was finding out whether or not we could still hold services in our building. There was no way we could heat our sanctuary with space heaters because it was just too big, so I decided to try using one of our large classrooms as an alternative. We had a Salamander, which is a large industrial size electric heater. I put that in the large classroom and after a couple of hours it was plenty warm. So we put some of our pews, along with our music and sound equipment in the room, and that Sunday we had church. It was cramped, but it worked: being in that room never hindered the Spirit of God from moving. In fact, it actually brought us together in a unique way and revival continued.

The biggest challenge was how we would replace the boiler. I called a few heating contractors and got some quotes, and submitted one of them to our bank, but our loan request was denied. They said that our debt-to-income ratio was not strong enough. It didn't help that a couple of years before that we had gotten a loan for a new roof, which was very costly.

I began praying and seeking God for direction. I knew that when the children of Israel were in Egypt they had *not enough* — they had to make bricks out of straw. In the wilderness they had *just enough* — God rained down manna daily. In the promised land, however, they had *more than enough*. Our church had always had just enough, and God had always provided for us. My question to Him was this: "How do we move from *just enough* to *more than enough*?" The Lord began to talk to me about giving sacrificially to foreign missions, and He took me to the book of Philippians:

> *"But my God shall supply all your needs according to his riches in glory by Christ Jesus."*
> Philippians 4:19

That's a great promise from the word of God that we all love, but as I read it that day the Lord impressed on me that it was conditional. I noticed that in Philippians 4:15 Paul said, *"Now you Philippians know also, that in the beginning of the gospel, when I departed from Macedonia, no church communicated with me concerning giving and receiving, but ye only."* In other words, the church at Philippi was the only church at that time that supported the Apostle Paul as a foreign missionary. This in turn brought the financial blessing of God upon that church. I had always given to foreign missions and we had taken up special offerings at our church, but it was now time to get serious and take things to the next level. I felt the anointing as God was showing me these things.

On April 21st, 2018 the Lord confirmed his word to me. I was on my way to the hospital to visit a patient, and as I was walking through the parking lot I ran into Brother David Trammell. That meeting was not a coincidence, but a divine appointment. I began to tell him what our church was going through financially and what God was showing me in the scriptures about giving to missions. Brother Trammell began to encourage me that what I had received was from the Lord. He prophesied to me while in the parking lot that God was going to take care of us, and that it wasn't going to be hard on our church. To prove his point, he wrote me a check for our church in the amount of $100 as he told me that our interaction and this offering was a sign that God was going to bless us. Before cashing that check, I made a copy of it and kept it in one of my Bibles. In the days ahead I would often look at it and remember our conversation on that day, as God used Brother Trammell to boost my faith.

Brother Trammell also encouraged me to call Brother Jack Leaman and schedule him to conduct a Faith Promise service for our church. Faith Promise is a program that challenges church members to ask God how much they should commit to give monthly to foreign missions, then believe that God will provide that amount. Through Faith Promise, many churches, saints, and ministers have been amazingly blessed. Brother Leaman has written books describing the countless testimonies and miracles that people have experienced through the years. On Wednesday evening, May 2nd, 2018, I taught a Bible study to our church about sacrificial giving. I shared with them things that God had been showing me and the people received it wonderfully. There was a beautiful anointing on that message.

During the next few days a vicious, unclean spirit began to attack my mind. I'm not one to say that every bad thing that happens to me is from the enemy, and I don't look behind every bush or rock for the devil, but this was a spirit designed to intimidate me. It was telling me that giving to foreign missions was not being accepted by the whole church, some were disgruntled and this would split my church. In reality, I didn't sense that from any of the saints in our church and I knew this was surely a lie. You can tell when you're fighting an unclean spirit because it makes you feel like you've done something wrong when you haven't; it makes you feel guilty when you're innocent. The enemy likes to show up when he knows you're on the verge of a blessing. That's when you have to draw on your faith, put on the whole armor of God and stand against his tactics.

I went to the church, locked myself in my office, and had a little talk with Jesus. I had already scheduled Brother Leaman to come and preach at our church, so I prayed: "Lord, if it's your will for Brother Leaman to come to our church, then have somebody give me $500 as a confirmation." Before the week was out, there was a lady in our church that called me and said that the Lord had told her to give our church $500. She knew nothing of my battle with the enemy, nor did she know about my prayer. God is so good! If we will stand against the enemy and be strong in our faith the Lord will deal with our enemy and keep blessing us in the process.

On September 16th, 2018, Brother Jack Leaman came and held a Faith Promise service at our church. The people responded wonderfully and many financial commitments were made to foreign missions. Two days after that service, one of the ladies in my church called to give a testimony of how God had blessed her and her husband. She said they were perhaps the poorest family in our church and yet they felt led by God to commit to giving $50 per month. They really could not afford to give any money, but they stepped out in faith. She was so excited to tell me that one of their children had qualified to receive disability, which came out to $750 a month. This was a miracle because previously, the disability benefits had been denied. Additionally, they were also struggling to pay their mortgage and were worried about losing their house. Because of their obedience and God's faithfulness, they were now easily able to pay their mortgage, keep their house, and had extra money for other needs. A man that had left our church and had just started coming back spoke with me three days after that service. He told me that not only was he going to start coming back to church, but he was going to pay double tithes, plus give to foreign missions.

Eight days after the Faith Promise service, the Lord gave my wife a blessing. She had been searching for a part-time job and as she was walking through our local shopping mall, the owner of the health food store stopped her unprovoked and asked her if she wanted a job. She said she would be happy to take the job and he hired her on the spot and she started work the next day. She was also given a 30% discount on all of the items in the store, which helped us a great deal with all the supplements that I had been purchasing.

Not only were people giving more to missions, but our tithing increased as well. Sometimes pastors may be concerned that if their people give to missions, that their tithes will go down. I've learned first-hand that it actually works the other way around. When people start giving in one area, they tend to give in other areas. This is because giving doesn't actually start with our checkbook, it starts in our heart. When a person has a giving heart, they will easily give to the kingdom of God, regardless of the need.

It made me feel great as a pastor that our church had increased their giving, but as we entered into the winter season we still did not have a replacement for our boiler, so we once again held our services in the classroom that we had used the previous year. This was not something that I wanted to do, and I felt a little disappointed, but the people had a good understanding of the situation and we continued to have great services. On the inside, however, I was feeling the pressure to get the heating situation resolved. Despite the fact that we were seeing an increase in our giving, the bank still would not give us a loan. It was frustrating because the new system would only cost us about $200 extra per month.

A pastor can sometimes be his own worst enemy. He or she can put pressure on themselves and create their own stresses. By now, I'm sure you know that I am very good at that! I knew that eventually the situation would be resolved, but I was starting to feel like a bit of a failure, and I was getting worn down with the whole process. Remember that I was still battling fatigue and unbalanced hormone issues. It's hard enough to deal with problems and unresolved issues when you feel good, but when you don't feel well it can take its toll. My mind was starting to get tired and I started to feel that tightness in the left side of my chest again where I always carry stress. I remember being at the building one day by myself and feeling a lot of stress and fatigue, even breathing seemed difficult. I had a thought of what would happen if I had a heart attack. As I was walking down the hallway of our church the Holy Ghost suddenly spoke to me these words: *"I will be with you. I will give you strength when you need it. I will preserve you from having a heart attack."* As I write this it's been over three years since the Lord spoke that to me and almost every day I thank God for keeping me from having a heart attack. Men start to think about these things when they get in their 50s, but thank God we have a living Savior who helps us along our way.

While out walking one evening the Lord spoke to me again. This time he said, *"Take my yoke upon you."* That was it - short and sweet. I began to study that verse of scripture to find out exactly what it meant. In Biblical times they would yoke two oxen together to plow a field. Usually they would yoke an older ox with a younger. The purpose was so that the older could teach the younger. This is why Jesus said, *"Take my yoke upon you, and learn of me."* It can also be translated in Greek as "learn from me." In addition, the older ox would be much stronger than the younger and would be able to bear the load that the younger ox would struggle with. So being yoked together with Jesus is how he teaches us and helps carry our heavy load. I came to the conclusion that I was trying too much to figure things out, and carry things on my own. This always leads to pressure and stress, yet when He spoke those wonderful words to me He did so in such a loving gentle way. Our God never speaks with condemnation.

We got through the winter season without any problems and by spring, we were back in our sanctuary again. The year 2019 was a relatively easy year with no big mountains to climb nor any deep valleys to walk through, but I was still battling the health issues. When I had started on the testosterone cream in 2008, the doctor suggested that I take 100 mg per day, but I could never take that amount because I was so sensitive to it. I instead would usually take around 50 mg. It was in 2019 when I began to notice my body start tolerating the cream better, until eventually I was able to take 100 mg. What concerned me was that it didn't stop there. Gradually my body was needing more and more and by the end of the year I was taking 200 mg or more per day. I mentioned this to my doctor's office, but was told this is not uncommon because if you've taken testosterone cream over a lengthy period of time, your body can stop absorbing it into your bloodstream. Therefore you need to continue increasing your dose over time. I was also concerned because in spite of the increased doses, my testosterone levels were not going up like they should. In addition, I was also not feeling good mentally or emotionally. I just had a feeling that something was off. My doctor suggested that I try testosterone injections, which would go straight into my bloodstream, but I was reluctant to try that. An injection of testosterone can stay in your body for up to a week, so if you have too much and it makes you aggressive you have to deal with that for a full week. As a pastor and having to be around people that was not something that I considered a good idea. My wife and I would often discuss that I must have some underlying problem that the doctors had never discovered. In spite of having low testosterone levels, the rest of my labs all came back great. However, we both suspected that testosterone was not my only issue.

On September 15th, 2019 brother Jack Leaman came back to our church for another Faith Promise service. Again the people responded wonderfully and there was a beautiful anointing during the altar service. My wife and I increased our monthly commitment and trusted God to help us keep it. By the end of the month, the Lord surprised us with a huge blessing. A man called me and asked if he bought us a new car would we be able to make the insurance payments. Of course I said yes. We arranged to meet at the car dealership and on September 30th we were picked out a brand new 2019 Chevy Malibu with only 2,800 miles on the odometer. After the man purchased the car for us he said that he felt led by God to give us an additional $100 per month to cover the insurance. You can never out-give God!

As the winter of 2019 approached, we found ourselves having to leave our specious sanctuary and once again hold services in a classroom. This was the third year of having to do so and I was dreading it at this point. The people never complained, but I think they were ready for a change also. We took up heating pledges to show the bank that we had plenty of cash flow for a new furnace, but again, we were having a hard time getting the loan. On January 1st, 2020, we were still in the classroom with no loan, but I was not discouraged. I knew that somehow God was going to come through for us. If God could bless us with a new car, He could bless us with a new furnace. I went back in my mind to the prophecy that Brother David Trammell had spoken over me. He told me that God was going to take care of us and it would not be hard on our church. I would often look at the copy of the check that he'd written out for $100 on April 21st, 2018, lifting it up before the Lord and thanking Him for the blessing that was coming. I didn't know when or how, nevertheless, I had a sense in my spirit that there was a purpose in everything that we were going through. I began to notice that in spite of the fact that we didn't yet have an HVAC loan, our church had become a very generous and giving Church: *we had been transformed by our troubles*. We as Christians have to believe that there is a purpose in every trial. Sometimes God sends us into a test, a trial or a wilderness experience because he's trying to teach us something or graduate us to the next level of faith.

During the first few months of 2020, I was feeling quite strong in my preaching and prayer-time. The anointing was flowing and I felt good about the future. The Lord gave me a message that I preached on February 28th, 2020 at our sectional Unity Service entitled, "When Things Don't Turn Out As Expected." I don't know that that message was prophetic, but it sure described the way the rest of the year unfolded. I remember sitting on the platform next to Brother David Trammell and he was telling me how he just came home from Italy where there was a strange virus on the land called the Coronavirus. Little did any of us know that it would become a worldwide pandemic. The Covid-19 pandemic was not something that any of us would have predicted, and it impacted all of us in different ways. My heart goes out to those that have lost loved ones that were so dear to their hearts. It also brought a great deal of fear into our world and even into the church. For church leadership, it posed the challenge of how we would conduct church business and services with our churches shut down. I am sure I'm not the only pastor that was concerned about tithes and offerings, but I am grateful to report that I have heard the majority of churches everywhere experienced an increase in giving during the shutdown. This is nothing less than the blessing of God, and the faithfulness of God's people. It shows us that in these end times we need not fear what we will encounter or experience. The same God that provided for the children of Israel in the wilderness is with us in these end times. He will take care of His church.

On Wednesday March 18th, 2020, we canceled our midweek Bible study due to Covid-19, which seemed so strange. Before the pandemic hit we had never had an online ministry, but that Sunday March 22nd, 2020, we launched one on Facebook. It was very different for me having to preach to a camera with only a few people around and I missed my church family, and I know they all missed being together in the house of God. But our online ministry kept us connected.

We were closed down for a couple of months and did not open again until May 17th, 2020. During the two months we were shut down I noticed that I started feeling better emotionally, mentally and physically. I viewed those two months as a gift from God that allowed me to rest in ways I could not have rested otherwise. It made me realize how much goes into the typical service for a pastor. When I was preaching online I would just preach the lesson and then be done with it and go home, but so much more goes into a service when you are pastoring a church. Number one, you have to be there early. Then, there's sometimes people that need to talk, or unexpected problems to attend to. There's a certain amount of energy expended during the praise and worship service. Then comes the actual ministry of the word, but it doesn't stop there. Most shepherds get involved with the altar service; exhort people to pray, and lay hands on the flock, and pour themselves into the people. After the service is the high point of the week for most pastors. The message has been delivered; the people are blessed, but even then there can be more counseling that needs to be done before the pastor gets to go home.

Sundays are both emotionally energizing and draining days for people in the ministry. I remember reading somewhere that Monday is the day of the week where pastors are most likely to quit their ministry or have a heart attack. Here's a direct quote from an unidentified pastor: *"I resign from the church in my mind about 10 times a year. Every time, it has been on a Monday."* Pastors are also vulnerable just before or after their sermon. That's when a church member may say a negative or snarky comment that the pastor remembers on Monday morning. The pastor didn't have time to process that on Sunday so he may chew on that throughout the beginning of the week. Even though the Sunday service may have been a complete success, the pastor will sometimes let that one negative comment fester in his mind until he resolves it for himself. Sometimes church members treat their pastors like they're made of steel or concrete. Church members should remember that pastors are human beings just like everyone else. They have their own problems and emotions just like everyone else. Elijah the prophet was a man subject to like passions as we are. I have often wondered what would happen if every church member had the opportunity to pastor their church for 30 days? Then again, maybe every pastor should have the opportunity to sit in the pew for 30 days? If it were possible for us all to see things from each other's perspective, I believe it would bring a lot more patience, humility, and understanding into the church.

My point in saying all of that is that when our church was shut down for two months I didn't realize how taxing the job of pastoring really is. When our church opened back up in the month of May, I was so excited to see all of our church members, but it didn't take too long before I began to feel tired again. Please don't misunderstand me: I am not complaining, but merely stating my experience and how it affected me. It inspired me to try and find a way to rest while carrying the heavy load of the ministry. Jesus said his yoke is easy and his burden is light. Anytime it becomes hard and heavy then I think we need to examine ourselves. I for one know that I often try to carry too much on my own shoulders. I haven't got it all figured out yet, but I'm trying to learn.

As the winter of 2020 was approaching I asked my heating contractor what we could do to get enough heat to keep us in our sanctuary. He proposed installing two furnaces that would heat the sanctuary only, which cost $10,000. This left the rest of the building unheated, but at least we could hold services in our sanctuary. I contacted the UPC Loan Fund and was told that they had a Hurricane Relief Fund loan that went up to $10,000, which was exactly the amount we needed. We obviously didn't have any hurricane damage, but we did have what was considered an emergency, and they graciously extended us the loan. From there we prepared to refinance our mortgage with the UPC Loan Fund, which would include an HVAC loan for the rest of the building. In the spring we were approved for the loan and as I write this we now have a brand new HVAC system installed throughout our church. While it took us a few years to get this done it was not hard financially on our church. This fulfilled the prophecy that Brother David Trammell had spoken over me a few years before.

Brother Trammell served as the Michigan District Superintendent during many of these stories and references. I would like to give him honor for not only leading our District well, but for speaking faith into my church and life. Without Brother Trammell, it would have been very difficult to press on.

CHAPTER SIX
MY CALAMITY

*"He maketh the storm a calm,
so that the waves thereof are still."*
Genesis 15:13-14

When 2020 came to a close, I think that most everyone was glad to see it go and have a new year upon us. I was hopeful that 2021 would bring better things than the previous year, but 2021 proved to be an extremely difficult year for my wife and I, and our families. In fact I could probably write a whole book about 2021, by itself. Instead, I will summarize the events.

My father-in-law, Eddie Andrews, had been battling cancer for approximately two years. In February of 2020, we had a prayer meeting where God touched him and he was healed; we rejoiced and gave God the glory. After this prayer meeting, the x-ray showed that the tumor had actually shrunk and he was on the mend. Unfortunately, throughout much of November and December 2020 he began to fall ill again. In December, he was admitted to the hospital in our hometown of Jackson, Michigan. They soon discovered that he had AML (Acute Myeloid Leukemia), and our family was told he needed to be transported immediately to a hospital in Detroit to receive specialized care, otherwise he may not survive through the night. That was very difficult for us as we could not visit him there because of COVID-19 restrictions. During that time he suffered a stroke, kidney failure and a host of other problems. He remained in the hospital for a few months, but by the grace of God he was allowed to come home in the spring of 2021. On Easter Sunday he attended church where he actually played piano and sang with a fresh anointing. It was a wonderful Sunday service for our whole church. We were so thankful to see him and have him back. It was a boost to our faith.

During the beginning of 2021, I was still really battling with my health. I was having a lot of clamminess mostly in my back, and some chest pain on the left side of my ribs. At first I didn't think much of it because I knew in the past that whenever I was under a lot of stress, my body would feel clammy with tightness in the left side of my chest. However, this seemed more severe. On January 8th, 2021, my doctor did some x-rays which showed that my rib cage had shifted and was causing intercostal nerve pain. If the rib cage is twisted, it can aggravate surrounding nerves, cause chest discomfort and pain, and can make breathing difficult because of added pressure on the diaphragm and lungs. Many people go to the emergency room with these symptoms thinking they are having a heart attack. The doctor listened to my heart and said it was strong, and that my lungs sounded great! What I really needed was some good old-fashioned rest.

One week later, I was speaking with a pastor friend of mine and he brought up the subject of taking weekly Sabbaths. He did not realize it, but he was the third pastor in less than a year that had spoken to me regarding weekly Sabbaths. The Bible does say that in the mouth of two or three witnesses let every word be established, so I felt that this was God speaking to me. I began to study the subject and felt strongly persuaded that God wanted me to begin taking a weekly Sabbath. On February 4th, 2021, I did exactly that. Before taking my first Sabbath I had informed the church of what God had been dealing with me about and actually taught a lesson about the importance of rest. I told them that every Thursday would be my day off and that I would return any calls the following day, unless it was an emergency. They actually applauded when I made this announcement, which encouraged me greatly. An excellent resource on this subject is a book written by Robert Morris entitled, "*Take the Day Off*". I would strongly recommend that book to every pastor or minister that wants to learn more. As I began to take weekly Sabbaths I noticed that I was feeling better, the chest pain subsided and I felt more creative in my mind and spirit.

Meanwhile, my father-in-law was still having his health battles. It was good to have him home, but he was obviously declining. He was losing weight and his strength was not coming back. Trying to move around with a walker was becoming increasingly difficult. The doctor ran a scan and discovered that the tumor in his colon had returned, and my father-in-law immediately opted out of chemotherapy and radiation treatments. Unless God performed a miracle of healing, he only had about six months left to live. During his life, he had prayed for more than one person that was on their deathbed and saw God raise them to good health and strength, so his faith was strong. We prayed, knowing that as long as there's breath in the body there's hope that God can bring healing. While we knew that death was a possibility, the wonderful thing about being a Christian is that even in death we have victory. The apostle Paul said, *"to live is Christ, and to die is gain."* When a Christian is absent from their body they are present with the Lord. We knew that if my father-in-law did not get his healing that he was ready to meet the Lord, which is the ultimate healing. That is a huge comfort to the family when they have a loved one who is so sick.

Debbie and I had a discussion about my own health, and we both agreed that 2021 needed to be a year of answers for me. I scheduled an appointment in April with my doctor at the Born Clinic and asked him to run as many tests on me as deemed necessary, as chronic fatigue and brain fog was making it difficult to function. I was still able to pray, study my Bible, preach sermons and take care of my church duties, but it was such a struggle to do simple things. I told my doctor that I needed some answers regarding testosterone. At that point I had been using the testosterone cream for nearly thirteen years, but as I said earlier, I was having to take more and more because it was not being absorbed through my skin into my bloodstream. Something had to change. This time when my doctor spoke about testosterone injections I felt that it was time to give it a try. He wanted to start me off with an injection of 100 mg, but I was a little reluctant and asked him to start out with 50 mg. I tolerated that dose very well without feeling aggressive, so after a few weeks I gradually increased to a weekly dose of 200 mg. I soon noticed that my skin no longer felt clammy and my mind felt clearer. I wasn't 100%, but I felt much better than when I was on the cream. A few weeks later I had some lab work done and my total testosterone levels were over 1,000 ng/dl, which was very good.

On Saturday, April 17th, my wife and I went to the church to pray, which we always do for the upcoming Sunday service. She is very sensitive to the Spirit and that evening God gave her a prophetic word - "*Storm.*" The Lord didn't give her any details, but she was troubled in her spirit. In fact, we could both feel in the Spirit that something was going on, an undercurrent of some kind.

The next day I preached a strong message to our church about the rapture entitled, "*Get Right or Get Left.*" I felt a strong anointing to preach against sin and it upset one of our young people, but thankfully the parents and grandmother stood with me and told me that I had preached the word of God. A week later things were fully resolved with the young person and they are still in church. I told Debbie afterward that she was right about the storm, thinking that this situation was it. However, she informed me that the storm was still yet to come.

In the beginning of the month of May, the storm came. My dad began to lose weight and was having trouble swallowing. He went to the hospital and they treated him for dysphagia, which is a swallowing disorder. The procedure helped him temporarily, but he continued to have problems. On May 20th he went back to the hospital because he had no control over his bowels. After running several tests, they began to suspect cancer. Eleven days later, Dad's doctor called me with a medical update: he informed me that his CEA (Carcinoembryonic Antigen) level was 4,000 nanograms per milliliter. For reference, he said the normal range for CEA is 0 - 2.5 nanograms per milliliter of blood and anything greater than 10 ng/dL suggests extensive disease. Levels greater than 20 ng/dL suggests the spreading of cancer. After receiving that report, I was numb. Later that day I went to my parents' home and gave my dad the news, which was one of the most difficult things I have ever done in my life. I get choked up just writing about it.

On Tuesday, June 1st, I took my dad to the hospital for a liver biopsy. He was much too weak to walk at this point and needed to use a wheelchair. I can still remember sitting with him in the waiting room and most of the time he was too weak to even lift his head. When they called him back to start the procedure, I stayed with him for a while. When he had to take his shirt off and put on a hospital gown I was shocked at how thin he had become. You always view your parents as strong, and it is hard to see them become weak.

On Wednesday, June 3rd, I went to pick up my dad at his house for another doctor's appointment. On the way to the car he was walking with a cane, but looking very feeble. I offered to help him, but he insisted that he could do it himself. He told me to go in the house and get the wheelchair. I left him for just a moment and when I came back outside he had fallen face down in the grass and was not moving. I was careful not to move him since I didn't know if there were any broken bones and we called an ambulance and had him transported to the hospital. I can't describe the sorrow I felt for him that day; my heart broke to see my dad suffering like that.

I stayed with him at the hospital for about four hours before one of my aunts came to relieve me. I had to leave because I was teaching Bible study that night, but during my visit with my dad I was able to talk to him about the Lord. I told him that as concerned as I was for his sickness I was more concerned about his soul. My dad had grown up in church when he was younger and was baptized, but had not attended church for several years. I told him the importance of being ready should he not make it. I made sure that he knew that no one goes to Heaven just because you're a good person, but that Jesus is the way, the truth and the life and that no man comes to the Father but by Him. I stressed the need to repent and have his sins forgiven.

My dad was admitted to the hospital that evening. The next day Debbie and I, our daughter Marissa, my mom and his siblings were with him when he received the diagnosis of stage 4 cancer. It was in his liver but had metastasized throughout his body. We all made the decision that sending him to a hospice home would be best, so he could receive the specialized care that he needed. When all of the family had left we stuck around to talk with him. I reminded him about our conversation the previous day concerning the Lord. My dad was a different man that day. He told us that he'd been praying and talking to the Lord and I knew that he had sincerely repented. My dad is not the type to just say something like that unless he really means it, so that gave us great peace.

On Saturday, June 5th, I visited my dad at the hospice home. He had great difficulty in speaking to me, but was able to communicate a little bit. I talked about growing up as a child and what it was like to have him as a dad. I brought up memories of camping together as a family, and showed him an old scrapbook of drawings I'd done as a kid.

I still believed that God could heal my dad. There was no doubt in my mind. I've seen God do too many great things to doubt, but I also knew that if God did not give my dad a miracle he would not be with us for long, so I wanted to make sure that I left nothing unsaid. I told my dad that in life you don't get to pick your father, but that I had been given a good one. He told me that I'd been a good boy. I will treasure that moment forever. It's something that money can't buy.

On Sunday, June 6th, I preached a message to our church entitled, *"Do You Need a Miracle?"* Sometimes preachers get their messages because of what they are going through, and oftentimes God allows preachers to go through certain things so they can minister to their flock. We had a wonderful service that day and many people got blessed. I walked out of there with my faith high and still believed that my dad would get his miracle.

After church, I visited my dad and he was too weak to speak. I stayed with him for a while and then decided to go home and let him get his rest. Late that evening, around 10 pm, I felt the need to go back and see him again. This time I took Debbie and Marissa with me. When we arrived he was no longer responding. I held his hand and said, *"Dad if you can hear me, squeeze my hand,"* but there was no response. We decided it was time to pray. As we begin to call upon the name of Jesus you could literally feel the presence of God fill that room. The Holy Ghost rested on us for a good 20 to 30 minutes. During that prayer the power of God was so strong that it would not have surprised me had my dad set up in bed. While I was praying my wife witnessed something that I did not see. My dad, who had not been moving earlier, was waving his hands in what looked like an expression of praise and his mouth was moving. What was happening to my dad at that moment is something we will never know, but what we do know is that there was no doubt that God was in the room. When we left we had such a great peace and an overwhelming feeling of joy.

While sleeping that night, my mom called me and said that the hospice home had called to say that Dad was close to leaving us. I went and picked her up and we went to be with him. Dad passed away at 3:05 am on Monday, June 7th, 2021. This was the storm that the Lord has spoken to my wife and I about. It was all a whirlwind and it happened so fast it was hard to comprehend that it had really happened. Just 30 days before, my dad had just begun to lose weight and have swallowing problems. Now, he was gone.

Sometimes when you are going through a storm, you may think it has finally ended, only for it to surge again. Before I had time to really grieve my dad, most of our time and energy was turned toward my father-in-law. He was getting weaker by the day and we found ourselves only in the eye of our storm. It's been said that the eye of the storm is the calm at the center of the storm; it's a place of strange peace. Despite all that we were going through, we felt that wonderful peace that only comes from the presence of God. My father-in-law also felt that peace. The three of us felt that everything was in God's hands, and that God would work all things together for good. Throughout the month of June he came to church when he could, but he needed to be pushed to the platform in a wheelchair. Despite his feeble condition, he still insisted on playing piano and singing. The Holy Ghost would come upon him and we were amazed how God gave him strength in those moments, but he was really struggling.

He soon became bedridden and July 11th was his last church service. A couple of weeks later we all decided it was best to place him in the hospice home; the same exact place that my dad had been. With the memories of my dad so fresh in my mind, and having not had time to grieve for him, it was difficult to step foot back in that place. On August 6th my father-in-law, Eddie Andrews, passed away. He served God as our original piano player and had ministered for 60 years. What an amazing example of faithfulness and loyalty he was. Eddie was very special to me and I will never forget him. When Debbie and I were newlyweds, I was brand new in the church, and I would sit with him and ask him question after question about the church, the Bible, and whatever came to mind. He was so willing and patient to pour into me his many years of wisdom and knowledge. When I started my ministry he was my biggest supporter who would encourage me when I did right, and correct me when I did wrong. To this day, I find myself truly grateful for all of those moments. In the early days of my walk with God he was like scaffolding to a building that is being erected; he was there for me until I could stand on my own. From then on, he had a humorous way of reminding me not to think of myself more highly than I ought to think. I preached his funeral service, an honor and memory I will cherish.

Was the storm over? That was the question asked by Debbie and I. We never dreamed that we would lose our dads exactly 60 days apart. It was a surreal feeling. When you suffer losses of people that you love so much it makes you take a different view on life. I'm not saying that it made us paranoid, or fearful, but it made us realize how fragile life is. It births in you a compassion that is close to the heart of God. Have you ever seen images of people walking through their property after a tornado has hit, and they are searching through the wreckage looking for valuables? That's how it can feel when you've lost loved ones that were so dear to your heart. It makes you realize what is truly valuable in life: relationships with people, and especially with God.

As time moved forward, the storm clouds lifted and the strong winds stopped blowing. It was time to heal and get back to normal living, or at least try, but things had changed so much that normal wasn't normal anymore. I would go to my mom's house and expect to see my dad, but he wasn't there. Debbie would think about picking up the phone to call her dad, like she had done every day before, but he wasn't home. The storm was over, but our lives would never be the same. As I come to this point in the book my mind goes back to Job. It was a storm that took his ten children. He had also lost his finances, and was soon to lose his health, but in the midst of the storm's aftermath he found the most valuable thing in his life was still there: his worship to God.

"Then Job arose, and rent his mantle, and shaved his head, and fell down upon the ground and worshipped, And said, Naked came I out of my mother's womb, naked shall I return thither: the LORD gave, the LORD hath taken away: blessed be the name of the LORD."
Job 1:20-21

As you can imagine, all of the grief and loss we had been through took its toll on us physically, mentally, and emotionally. We were absolutely wiped out. We tried to take care of ourselves and relax as much as we could, avoiding unnecessary things, but there are a lot of loose ends to tie up when you've lost loved ones. I became very busy with my mother, helping her to get her affairs in order; and Debbie was very busy helping her brother prepare to sell her dad's house.

After a few weeks we decided I needed to once again focus on my health battles. I scheduled another appointment at the Born Clinic. Since my testosterone levels had been so good, we agreed that it might be best to get tested again for candida and food sensitivities. The results came back that my candida levels were indeed very high, and I had several food sensitivities. This meant that I had to become serious about my diet. I had to avoid all sugar, yeast and preservatives if I wanted to start feeling better. As I stated earlier in the book, I had an overgrowth of candida in my gut. In other words: a yeast infection. It can be very difficult to get rid of this condition. Many people have tried for years, even decades, without success. I decided to follow my doctor's instructions thoroughly, but also do all of the research that I could do on my own. This was my Goliath, and it was standing in the way of my destiny. I was not, however, discouraged by any of this. It was actually encouraging to have something with a name on it that I could fight. God knows that I'm a fighter. The word *quit* is not in my vocabulary. Greater is He that is in me, than he that is in the world!

On September 19th, 2021, we held a Back To School Children's Service. I invited Brother Anthony Miller and his wife Danielle to minister. It was their first time at our church and we had a wonderful time, with both young and old participating. After service we went out for food and fellowship and enjoyed getting to know them and their family. We now count them as some of our dearest friends. During our meal I briefly mentioned to Brother Miller about my health battles, and made the statement that I'd often thought of writing a book. He became interested and told me that he had already helped Sister Rebecca Trammell edit and publish two books, and that he could help me in writing a book. I think his exact words were, "Let's do it!" That's how this whole book came to fruition. As we spoke that day I really felt it was the timing of God that this book be written, and I still feel today that everything that I have been through has been for a purpose, and is perhaps meant to help others in their journey. This book is the book that I wish had been written for me when I was struggling. My hope is that someone will find strength and encouragement to keep going; to keep believing that God is with you; and that He has a purpose.

October 20th, 2021, I preached at a funeral service for a 29-year old man that died instantly from a massive heart attack. I did not know this man nor his family, but was asked by one of the men in my church to do the funeral for his brother. With all of the grief I had been through you would think that would have been an extremely hard service for me, but in a strange way it made it easier. I've done more funerals than I can count, but in that service I felt more compassion for that family than ever. It's true what the Bible says: sorrow makes the heart better. It is our suffering that makes us able to minister to people in their heartache. You can't really minister to somebody's pain unless you have felt that pain yourself. Brother Teets used to say that the shepherd cannot minister to the sheep in the valley unless he first goes through the valley himself. We as ministers do our best to avoid suffering just like anyone else, but if we are truly going to be anointed and bring a healing virtue to others, we will have to suffer as Christ suffered. There's no doubt that a genuine Holy Ghost anointing is extremely expensive. It takes more than prayer and fasting to be truly anointed; it takes suffering. When Jesus really wants to use you He will let you suffer first. Suffering takes your anointing to the next level. Yet while you are suffering, don't forget about His grace!

> *"But the God of all Grace, who has called*
> *us unto his eternal glory by Christ Jesus,*
> *after that you have suffered a while,*
> *make you perfect, establish, strengthen, settle you."*
> 1 Peter 5:10

As 2021 was coming to a close, I began to prepare mentally for my Candida Diet. I began to slowly give up some of the bad foods and replace them with good choices. I decided that I would not go into this 100% until after the holidays were completely over. Too many temptations! I also had to tell the church to please not bring me sweets. I have some ladies in my church that have always spoiled me with cookies, cheesecakes, pies and breads. This was going to be a lifestyle change. I also discovered some excellent products that can help remove bad things out of your gut and restore good bacteria that are so desperately needed for good health.

You may be wondering, "Did he ever get well?" All I can tell you is that I started 2022 feeling very optimistic about my health. I wasn't eager to give up the fast foods and the sweets, but I was looking forward to getting a handle on my health problems. As I am writing this, I have gone nearly two months without any sugar, or junk food of any kind. My mind has felt clearer and I can feel that my body is slowly changing. It takes a long time to get sick, and it can take just as long to get healthy, but mentally I was ready to do whatever it took to get well. When a preacher doesn't feel good he may feel like there's a preacher inside of him screaming to get out. He can sense the anointing, but his body doesn't want to cooperate. At least that's how I have often felt. Now, however, I have more hope than ever before that I would finally turn the page on so many things that I had battled in the past.

On January 16th, 2022 Bishop McKinnies preached at our church. He preached: *"What Great Things Are You Expecting From the Lord This Year?"* What a great title! After the service I was telling Bishop and Sister McKinnies about the book I was writing. When I was asked what the book was about, I said that I was thinking of calling it *Afflicted*, and using it to describe how afflictions can fulfill

God's purpose in our life. Sister McKinnies suggested the title *Embracing Afflictions*. I immediately fell in love with that title and ran with it. I have to give her credit for the name of this book.

The very next Sunday, which was January 23rd, I preached from that title: *Embracing Afflictions*. Many were blessed when I preached it, so I chose to include that sermon in the next chapter of this book, also because it sums up everything I've been trying to say from the beginning. I chose not to make it a literal transcription, but rather changed it a little bit to fit in book form. I hope you are blessed and encouraged as you read it.

However, before moving into the sermon there is something that I've been wanting to say. I have not spoken much in this book about my marriage. As you can imagine, all that I've been through has not been easy for me or my wife. However, I honestly can say that it has made my wife and I closer than ever before. It has made us more than just husband and wife. I can honestly say that she is my best friend and my biggest supporter. I love her now more than ever and I thank God that she is in my life. I can't imagine what I would ever have done without her. She's been my rock and I hope we have many more years together. Thank you, Debbie. You're the best!

CHAPTER SEVEN
EMBRACING AFFLICTIONS

"And the patriarchs, moved with envy, sold Joseph into Egypt; but God was with him, and delivered him out of all his afflictions, and gave him favor and wisdom in the sight of Pharaoh king of Egypt; and he made him governor over Egypt and all his house."
Acts 7:9-10

Afflictions are also known as hardships or troubles. They are something that we pray for God to deliver us from and are certainly not enjoyable – so why would we want to *embrace* afflictions? We must understand first that afflictions are going to come whether we want them or not. Secondly, it was David in Psalm 119:71 that said, *"It is good for me that I was afflicted; that I might learn thy statutes."* In this light, we understand that good can come out of our afflictions, however, this requires that we have the right mindset. Thank God that His word is a lamp to our feet and a light unto our path, and it helps us to be transformed in our thinking so that we can see things from His perspective instead of ours. From God's perspective, He is always developing us and working for our good, though sometimes it doesn't feel like it.

The patriarchs were Joseph's older brothers. They *moved with envy* against him, which means they were extremely jealous, even to the point of hatred. In reading the scripture we can discover where their jealousy stemmed from.

> *"Now Israel loved Joseph more than all his children, because he was the son of his old age: and he made him a coat of many colours. And when his brethren saw that their father loved him more than all his brethren, they hated him, and could not speak peaceably unto him. And Joseph dreamed a dream, and he told it his brethren: and they hated him yet the more."*
> Genesis 37:3-5

Israel was also known as Jacob. God changed Jacob's name when they wrestled and God blessed him in Genesis 32. It seems that Jacob loved Joseph more like a grandson than a son. Parents love their children, but they spoil their grandchildren, and Jacob showed Joseph favoritism by making him a coat of many colors. Some think that the coat represented the fact that Joseph received the birthright. He was Rachel's first born son, but the youngest of all his brothers. They became so insanely jealous of him that they sold him into slavery.

> *"And it came to pass, when Joseph was come unto his brethren, that they stript Joseph out of his coat, his coat of many colours that was on him; and they took him, and*

cast him into a pit: and the pit was empty, there was no water in it. And they sat down to eat bread: and they lifted up their eyes and looked, and, behold, a company of Ishmeelites came from Gilead with their camels bearing spicery and balm and myrrh, going to carry it down to Egypt. And Judah said unto his brethren, What profit is it if we slay our brother, and conceal his blood? Come, and let us sell him to the Ishmeelites, and let not our hand be upon him; for he is our brother and our flesh. And his brethren were content. Then there passed by Midianites merchantmen; and they drew and lifted up Joseph out of the pit, and sold Joseph to the Ishmeelites for twenty pieces of silver: and they brought Joseph into Egypt."
Genesis 37:23-28

"And Joseph was brought down to Egypt; and Potiphar, an officer of Pharaoh, captain of the guard, an Egyptian, bought him of the hands of the Ishmeelites, which had brought him down thither. And the Lord was with Joseph, and he was a prosperous man; and he was in the house of his master the Egyptian. And his master saw that the Lord was with him, and that the Lord made all that he did to prosper in his hand.
Genesis 39:1-3

When you are suffering affliction, I suggest four things you need to believe:

1. God is with you.
2. All things work together for good.
3. Your relationship with God matters.
4. God has a purpose in your pain.

When Joseph's brothers became jealous and sold him into slavery, the Bible declares that God was with him. (*Acts 7:9*) God was also with him as a slave, and later when he was cast into prison. (*Genesis 39:2-3, 21-23*) Did you know that God can be with you and yet you do not sense His presence? I'm sure you have experienced that if you've walked with God for any time. We as Holy Spirit-filled believers love to feel the presence of God, but sometimes the presence of God seems to have evaporated. While we still have our faith as we walk through dry seasons, we may wonder why God's presence seems to be absent. Where is the anointing that allows me to sense the nearness of God's presence? It's worth noting that when Joseph's brothers cast him into a pit there was no water, as they were often old cisterns without water used to keep prisoners in. He was a dreamer in a dry place. Sometimes we may find ourselves in a pit – not literally, but figuratively. It could be a pit of discouragement, sorrow, financial struggle, marital struggle, or sickness. Water is often symbolic of the manifest presence of God: Jesus said out of your belly shall flow rivers of living water, but this spake He of the Spirit. When I view Joseph being in a pit with no water, it paints a picture for me of a believer being in a discouraging situation and having a

dryness in their spirit; not being able to feel the presence of God. Maybe you are in a pit and cannot sense the presence of God. In that case I encourage you to believe that God is still with you. The scripture declares that God is a *very present* help; not a help *on the way*. That means that He is with you. He said I will never leave thee, nor forsake thee.
I heard a story of a woman who had a dream where she saw three women kneeling at an altar praying. She watched as the Lord came to the first woman, laying His hand on her head and whispered something in her ear. To the second woman, He simply laid His hand on her head, but said nothing. To the third woman He stood far off without touching her nor speaking to her. The woman that had the dream said to the Lord, "The first woman must be really pleasing to you. You touched her and spoke to her so intimately, but the last woman must have done something to disappoint you, because you stood far off." Jesus told the woman that she had misinterpreted the dream: the first woman had very immature faith and needed, like a baby, to be constantly touched and reassured; but the third woman had such mature faith that she did not need the constant touch and reassurance of His presence. This type of faith pleased Him most of all. Without feeling His presence or hearing His voice, she simply believed that He was with her.

You must believe that **God is with you!**

God eventually delivered Joseph out of all of his afflictions. He was thrown in the pit at the age of 17, (*Genesis 39:24*) and it wasn't until age 30 that he stood before Pharaoh, king of Egypt (*Genesis 41:46*). That's 13 years of affliction! Yet through every solitary, confusing moment, God was with him. God gave him two things: favor and wisdom in the sight of Pharaoh, who made him governor over Egypt and all his house.

Once believing that God is with you, you must believe that **all things work together for good!** (*Romans 8:28*). God took Joseph's dreams, his brother's jealousy, the pit, the accusations of Potiphar's wife, the prison, and worked all of those things together for good. When Joseph was reunited with his brothers years later he did not blame them. Instead, he said: *"God did send me before you to preserve life."* (Genesis 45:5). *"Ye thought evil against me, but God meant it unto good."* (Genesis 50:20). If we believe that God makes all things work together for good, it makes it easier to forgive those who have hurt us or betrayed us. We can see that even they were part of God's plan to bring about good in our lives. He prepares a table before us in the presence of our enemies, He anoints our head with oil, and our cup runneth over.

As I have been writing this book, I've been able to look back and see how God has orchestrated bad things in my life for good. I'm hoping that you can do the same, but also that your eyes are becoming open to view your present struggles as being future victories. Can you look at your present problems and see that they will one day work for good? Can you stand at your Red Sea and say, *"Stand still and see the salvation of the Lord?"* Can you walk up the mountain and say, *"God himself will provide a sacrifice?"* Can you look at your situation and say, *"God will make a way where there is no way?"* Can you look at your pain and declare that this *will* work for your good?

> *"And we know that all things work together for good to them that love God, to them who are the called according to his purpose."*
> Romans 8:28

We should remember that Romans 8:28, as wonderful as it is, is not a blanket promise to the entire human race. There is an address on the envelope, so to speak. It is addressed *"to them that love God."* According to Jesus, those that love Him are those that have His commandments, and keep them. Those that do not keep His sayings do not love him. (*John 14:21, 24*). There's an old song that says, *"I told Him I loved Him, it was easy to say, but harder to prove it when temptation came my way."* When Potiphar's wife said to Joseph, *"Lie with me,"* Joseph responded by saying, *"How then can I do this great wickedness, and sin against God?"* Consider that Joseph was in a heathen nation, and those that worshiped Jehovah were nowhere to be found. Joseph still had his dreams, but they had not yet come to fruition. At that point in his life, living for God had not yet paid off. He could have committed sin and no one would have ever known, yet he still believed that his relationship with God mattered.

Your relationship with God matters!

You and I should value our relationship with God more than any other relationship. It's strange to me that some people blame God or walk away from him when things get bad. This is so foolish, and it is exactly what Satan wants! If you don't have a relationship with God, then the devil doesn't have to fight you. You have opposed yourself! We need to remember that our relationship with God is how we're going to get out of our afflictions.

> *"Many are the afflictions of the righteous:*
> *but The LORD delivereth him out of them all."*
> Psalm 34:19

For every affliction, there is a deliverance. When Job suffered his afflictions, he kept his integrity. He kept his relationship with God alive. Job said, *"Neither have I gone back from the commandment of his lips; I have esteemed the words of his mouth more than my necessary food."* (Job 23:12). He kept trusting in God, and looked for the day that God would deliver him. When Paul and Silas were beaten and thrown into prison, at midnight they prayed and sang praises to God. I encourage you in your affliction to keep your focus on your relationship with God. I know how easy it is to spend all of our time and energy focusing on the negative, the storm, the pain, the unending crisis, but God is there with you. Spend time in His word reading and meditating; spend time in prayer, praising Him, seeking Him, and listening for what He might say.

> *"Thou art near, O LORD;*
> *and all thy commandments are truth."*
> Psalm 119:151

Finally, Joseph's story teaches us that **God has a purpose in your pain**! When God began giving Joseph dreams at the age of 17 he was *calling* him according to His purpose. *(Romans 8:28)*. God's purpose supersedes all of our plans and imaginations. When God begins to work in our lives he unfolds things in His way, not ours. God had plans for Joseph to be the governor over Egypt, but God had to get Joseph from his father's house into the palace. So God began to order his steps. The first step was those wonderfully anointed dreams that captured Joseph's imagination and bolstered his faith. But the next steps included one painful circumstance after another—his brother's jealousy, the pit, slavery, Potiphar's wife, and the prison, but there was purpose in everything that Joseph suffered. With every step God was preparing him to rule and reign. With every step God was bringing him closer to the throne. If you take out any of those steps, then Joseph would never have seen his dreams fulfilled.

I believe the same is true in my life and yours. God has a purpose and a plan for our lives, and according to His sovereignty He orders our steps. The steps at times may be painful, or lonely, or extremely trying to our soul. We may even question the steps, but we have to trust God and believe that with every step He is leading us somewhere. Not just anywhere, but to a wonderful place in the kingdom of God. As tempting as it might be, you don't want to take out any of the steps, for then you would never get to where God is taking you. I challenge you to thank God and praise Him for whatever step you are on. Believe that God is with you, that all things work together for good, that your relationship with God matters, and that God has a purpose in your pain.

> *"The steps of a good man are ordered by the Lord:*
> *and he delighteth in his way."*
> Psalm 37:23

In conclusion, I am sure that somebody reading this has had to walk some difficult steps. Your steps have not been without tears, pressures, losses, or feelings of frustration, but let me encourage you to keep walking by faith, and not by sight. Don't forget the One who is ordering your steps. He has walked this way before you. He came as the Word made flesh. He was God Almighty, yet He experienced life from the human point of view. Christ also suffered for us, leaving us an example, that you should follow His steps. And He can be touched with the feeling of your infirmities, which simply means He knows how you feel. Let me encourage you by saying prophetically that one day the steps will change. When the trumpet sounds your steps will be lifted to a higher dimension. One day soon the church will be caught up to meet Jesus in the air! We will see Him with His eyes as a flame of fire, and His feet like polished brass. To His faithful he will say, *"Well done!"* And somewhere along the line we will find the steps leading us to the marriage supper of the Lamb, which will usher in the millennial kingdom of Jesus Christ. It's not time to stop walking with God, there's too much awaiting us in the future. It's time for you to embrace your afflictions and see the mighty hand of God in your life.

EMBRACING AFFLICTIONS

Made in the USA
Monee, IL
25 June 2022